From Garden to Table

FROM GARDEN TO TABLE

MARY NORWAK

Elm Tree Books/London

First published in Great Britain 1977
by Elm Tree Books/Hamish Hamilton Ltd
90 Great Russell Street London WC1B 3PT

Copyright © 1977 by Mary Norwak

SBN 241 89593 6

Jacket design and illustrations
by Maureen Roffey

Filmset and printed in Great Britain by
BAS Printers Limited, Over Wallop, Hampshire

Contents

Introduction

During the last year or two, there has been a revived interest in growing vegetables and fruit, greater than anything seen since the 1939–45 War when 'digging for victory' was essential. Now once again, we fight for economic survival, and family budgets are balanced by supplies of home produce.

But there are marvellous side-effects from growing one's own fruit and vegetables. Of course, the person who actually does the digging and hoeing benefits physically from hard outdoor work, and also benefits mentally from the interest in planning, reading gardening books and studying new methods. More important still, the whole family is able to enjoy really fresh produce, full of flavour, and packed with protein, calcium and a multitude of vitamins and minerals. Organically-grown vegetables undoubtedly have better flavour, lettuces and carrots keep fresher and potatoes don't bruise, and all vegetables have a firmer texture since their cell structure is thicker.

A well-planned garden completes our disillusionment with today's bland, processed food, because everyone quickly recognises the joy of full-flavoured food which has a 'crunchy' texture and rich natural colours to stimulate the appetite. In this book, I have tried to combine many favourite old recipes and ideas for using vegetables with some new and stimulating ways of incorporating the newly-popular sprouting seeds, beans and herbs into our diet.

A note on basic vegetable cooking

There is nothing more beautiful to look at, nor delicious to taste, than vegetables fresh from the garden, so it is worth taking a little extra care in cooking them and giving them the respect they deserve. This can mean quite a revolution in eating habits, discarding the notion that vegetables are just extra bulk to be quickly boiled and put on the plate alongside some meat or fish dish. Vegetables are beautiful enough to be enjoyed in their own right, to be cooked carefully as accompaniments to other foods, or to be presented proudly as complete dishes.

Break away from the routine of serving a salad only from conventional salad vegetables, or offering just one vegetable and potatoes at every meal. Try eating almost any vegetable raw for a change—both texture and flavour can be a revelation. Or serve three or four different vegetables for a meal, each cooked separately and dressed with butter and an appropriate herb. You can make a complete meal from vegetables, but if you feel you have to eat meat, try fresh vegetables with just a grilled bacon rasher or a piece of cold ham, both of which seem to go with everything and bring out vegetable flavours. Use leftover cooked vegetables in salads, convert them quickly into soup, or use them to fill pies or flans. Above all, think seriously of having one completely vegetable and fruit meal each day to aid digestion and improve your general health, as well as balancing the budget.

Vegetables should be eaten fresh and young, for nothing will restore the flavour of old stale produce. When the garden is in full production, harvest vegetables regularly, early in the day. Take what is needed for immediate use, and freeze or process surplus at once. Never leave vegetables to accumulate until there are glut quantities to tackle, or produce is too mature.

Prepare just as many vegetables as you need for the meal, unless you have plans for a cooked salad in the immediate future. Careful cooking retains the food value of vegetables and ensures a good supply of vitamins and minerals. Vegetables should be just tender, not soft and pulpy, and are best served immediately after cooking. *Boil* vegetables in just enough water to cover, lightly salted (avoid bicarbonate of soda). Cook until just tender (green vegetables are nicer when still slightly crisp), drain well and serve at once with a knob of butter. Many people prefer to *steam* vegetables instead of immersing them in water. Use a steamer, a colander standing in simmering water, or a double boiler, always ensuring that the top is tightly covered to catch the steam.

Braising conserves the flavour, and saves fuel when vegetables are cooked in the oven along with the main dish and a pudding. Put the vegetables into a tightly-lidded ovenware dish, and only just cover with water or stock, seasoned with salt and pepper. Allow 20–25 minutes in a moderate oven. The vegetables can be served in their juices, or these juices can be reduced by fast boiling in a clean saucepan to a glaze. Add a knob of butter to the glaze and pour over the vegetables before serving.

Stuffing need not be confined to the traditional marrow. Try filling cabbage, courgettes, cucumbers, aubergines or tomatoes with a meat, cheese or breadcrumb stuffing, with plenty of seasoning and herbs, and a home-made tomato or mushroom sauce, or gravy. A complete meal can be cooked in the oven if accompanying potatoes are baked in their jackets.

Roasting and Frying are particularly good for root vegetables. Boil potatoes, parsnips, Jerusalem artichokes, turnips or swedes for 5 minutes, then drain them well and put them round a joint, basting occasionally with

viii

the hot fat. When frying chips, cook them in hot clean fat until soft but pale. Remove from the fat for a few seconds, then plunge them back into the hot fat to become golden and crisp.

A note on the recipe measurements

Ingredients have been listed in both metric and imperial (in brackets) measures. It is most important to follow one set of measurements or the other, as they are not exact conversions. 25 g to 500 ml provides the same solid/liquid ratio as 1 oz to 1 pint; if the metric measures are followed, the recipe will yield about 10% less. Unless otherwise noted, each recipe will make enough for 4 people.

Vegetable ABC

ARTICHOKES (GLOBE)

These plants are highly decorative and the heads are delicious. They go stale very quickly and should be used immediately after cutting. Take off the outer leaves and trim the stalks. Leave the artichokes to soak, tips downwards, in plenty of cold water for an hour. Dig carefully into the artichokes and remove the hairy 'chokes', and trim the points from the leaves with sharp scissors. Put the artichokes into a large pan of lightly salted boiling water and boil gently for 40 minutes until a leaf pulls out easily. Drain well and serve hot with melted butter or Hollandaise sauce, or cold with French dressing or mayonnaise.

If you have a large number of artichokes, take off all the leaves, rub the hearts with lemon juice and cook them for 15 minutes. Serve the hearts in a salad mixed with mushrooms or seafood, or hot in a cheese sauce.

Artichokes Stuffed with Ham

4 globe artichokes
100 g (4 oz) cooked ham
50 g (2 oz) mushrooms
1 small onion

1 garlic clove
250 ml (½ pint) stock or white wine
50 g (2 oz) butter
salt and pepper

Cook the artichokes until just tender. Mince the ham and mix with the finely chopped mushrooms and onion, and crushed garlic. Fill the artichokes with the stuffing and put them into an ovenware dish with the stock or wine. Cover and bake at 180°C (350°F)/Gas 4 for 25 minutes. Put artichokes on serving plates. Melt the butter in the cooking liquid, season well and serve as a sauce.

ARTICHOKES (JERUSALEM)

These knobbly roots have the full flavour of globe artichoke hearts, and are very useful in the winter. They may be peeled, or boiled first and skinned when hot, and used for recipes in which artichoke hearts are specified, or for potato recipes. They are delicious baked around a joint of beef, or served as a creamy purée. A very good artichoke soup can be made by cooking the tubers in chicken stock, sieving and then thinning the purée with milk.

Artichokes with Cheese

675 g (1½ lb) Jerusalem artichokes
250 ml (½ pint) white sauce
salt and pepper
pinch ground nutmeg
75 g (3 oz) grated Cheddar cheese

Peel the artichokes and boil them in water to cover for 20 minutes. Drain, but keep 125 ml (¼ pint) cooking liquid. Cut the artichokes in slices and arrange them in a shallow ovenware dish. Mix the white sauce with the cooking liquid, season well with salt, pepper and nutmeg, and pour over the vegetables. Sprinkle on the cheese and grill until golden.

ASPARAGUS

Asparagus becomes stale quickly, so it must be cooked immediately after cutting. Grade the stalks for size before cooking. Trim off any woody portions and small scales, and tie into small bundles of even-sized spears. Cook in boiling water until just tender, standing the bundles in the pan, tips uppermost, so that the tips only steam while the stems are cooking more thoroughly. Start cooking thicker stalks first and add the bundles of thinner ones at intervals. Mix the sizes together before serving with melted butter, French dressing or Hollandaise sauce. A pinch of nutmeg helps to bring out the flavour. Cold asparagus can be served with French dressing and a sprinkling of sieved hard-boiled egg, or the tips may be dressed with mayonnaise or Hollandaise sauce.

Asparagus Flan

225 g (8 oz) shortcrust pastry
450 g (1 lb) asparagus
250 ml (½ pint) milk
3 eggs
salt and pepper
75 g (3 oz) grated Cheddar cheese

Line a flan ring or pie plate with the shortcrust pastry, prick well, line with foil and baking beans and bake at 200°C (400°F)/Gas 6 for 10 minutes. Cook and drain the asparagus and cut into 5-cm (2-in) lengths. Mix milk, eggs, salt and pepper and cheese. Put the asparagus into the pastry case, pour on the milk mixture and bake at 180°C (350°F)/Gas 4 for 30 minutes. Serve hot or cold.

AUBERGINES

Aubergines go particularly well with lamb, and partner onions, peppers and tomatoes in many recipes. Do not peel aubergines before cooking, but split them lengthwise or cut them across in slices. Sprinkle well with salt, leave to stand for an hour, and drain well before using. Aubergines are good stuffed with meat, vegetables and rice, and a tomato sauce is delicious with them. To serve as a plain vegetable, fry slices in oil, or dip them in batter and fry.

Ratatouille

4 tomatoes
2 aubergines
1 green pepper
2 medium-sized onions
2 courgettes
2 tablespoons olive oil
25 g (1 oz) butter
salt and pepper
1 garlic clove
parsley

3

Peel the tomatoes and slice them. Wipe and slice the aubergines. Remove the seeds from the green pepper, and slice. Slice the onions, and peel and slice the courgettes. Put oil and butter in heavy pan, heat and add vegetables, salt and pepper, and the crushed garlic clove. Stir well, and cover tightly. Simmer for 1 hour. When the dish is cooked, the vegetables should have absorbed all the oil. Garnish with chopped parsley and serve hot or cold.

Aubergine and Tomato Salad

4 aubergines
5 large tomatoes
1 tablespoon vinegar
1 teaspoon olive oil
salt and pepper

Put the aubergines on a baking sheet in a hot oven until their skins burst. Remove skins, and beat the pulp in a basin. Peel the tomatoes, chop roughly, and add to the aubergines. Mix vinegar, oil, salt and pepper and pour over the salad, tossing well.

BEETROOT

Beetroot is usually served as a salad, but it makes an excellent hot vegetable. Boiled beetroot may be served hot in a white sauce, or the beetroot may be cooled and sliced into vinegar. Try baking beetroot instead of boiling it to save all the flavour. Choose small beetroot of even size, wash them well, and leave about 2·5 cm (1 in) of the stems. Put into an ovenware dish without liquid, and bake at 180°C (350°F)/Gas 4 for 30 minutes, then at 160°C (325°F)/Gas 3 for 1 hour. When they are tender, peel the beetroot and serve with melted butter, salt and pepper.

Beetroot Soup

8 medium-sized beetroot
1 small onion
375 ml ($\frac{3}{4}$ pint) chicken stock
salt and pepper
juice of 1 lemon
1 tablespoon honey
pinch ground cloves

Wash the beetroot well and simmer until tender. Peel and sieve them with 250 ml ($\frac{1}{2}$ pint) cooking water. Mix with the remaining ingredients and simmer for 5 minutes. Serve plain, or with sour cream and chopped chives.

4

Beans

For full details of broad, French and runner beans, see Chapter 3.

Broccoli

The various types of broccoli are very popular and useful in the kitchen and it is one of the best vegetables to freeze. Cut the shoots cleanly with a knife, and if the lower stems are tough, peel them before cooking. Cook in boiling salted water for 10 minutes, and drain carefully so that the shoots do not break up. Broccoli is good served with melted butter or Hollandaise sauce, or it may be drained and dressed with French dressing for an unusual salad.

Brussels Sprouts

Use sprouts while they are small, firm and tightly closed, and bright green. Wash them well and cook in just enough water to float them. They are good on their own, but can be mixed with cooked chestnuts, or mushrooms, or onions, and are excellent in cheese sauce. Leftover sprouts can be covered with French dressing and mixed with a few nuts and a sprinkling of nutmeg for a salad, but raw shredded sprouts are also excellent as salad, particularly in a winter mixture with shredded leeks, celery and watercress. Don't waste the tops of the sprout plants. Remove them when all the sprouts have been harvested, cook them in boiling water, and serve with butter and plenty of seasoning.

Cabbage

There are so many varieties of cabbage that there is one in season at any time of the year. Crisp white-hearted cabbage makes wonderful salads when shredded raw, and even cooked cabbage should still have a slight 'bite' for the best texture and flavour. Really well-cooked cabbage needs no more than a dressing of butter, salt and pepper. Red cabbage is a splendid vegetable, because it makes a firm heart easily, and will stay in the ground during the winter months—it is delicious casseroled as an accompaniment to rich meats such as pork and duck.

Red Cabbage Casserole

1 small red cabbage
25 g (1 oz) dripping
1 medium-sized onion
1 apple
salt and pepper

5

flour
375 ml ($\frac{3}{4}$ pint) stock
3 tablespoons vinegar
pinch ground cinnamon
1 teaspoon sugar

Finely shred the cabbage. Melt the dripping, and add chopped onion and apple. Season with salt and pepper, sprinkle with a little flour, stir well and add cabbage. Pour on stock and vinegar, and cook with lid on at 180°C (350°F)/Gas 4 for 2 hours. Stir in cinnamon and sugar and serve hot.

CARROTS

Carrots are at their best when young and tender, cooked in very little water, but the older vegetables are an essential ingredient of winter casseroles and soups. Raw carrots are excellent, coarsely grated and dressed with lemon juice.

Carrots Vichy

450 g (1 lb) young carrots
65 g (2$\frac{1}{2}$ oz) butter
pinch salt
2 teaspoons sugar
1 tablespoon chopped parsley

Scrape the carrots and cut them into 0·5-cm ($\frac{1}{4}$-in) slices. Melt half the butter and add the salt, sugar and carrots. Add water just to cover, bring to the boil and simmer uncovered until the water has evaporated and the carrots are tender. This will take about 25 minutes. Add the remaining butter and sprinkle with finely chopped parsley before serving.

CAULIFLOWER

Cauliflowers are nicest cooked when they are still small and the curds are creamy-white and firm. To cook a whole cauliflower, cut a cross in the stem at the base and put into boiling water so that it comes just above the head. When the stem is just tender, the curds are cooked through. The cauliflower flowerets may also be broken off and cooked; this speeds up cooking for making soup, or the small pieces may be dressed in white or cheese sauce. The cauliflower leaves should not be wasted, but may be shredded (including the thick midrib) and cooked in boiling water, then served with butter and seasoning. A whole cauliflower makes a delicious dish on its own.

Cauliflower Polonaise

1 cauliflower
50 g (2 oz) butter
2 tablespoons fresh white breadcrumbs
1 hard-boiled egg
2 bacon rashers
1 dessertspoon chopped parsley

Trim the cauliflower and cook until tender. Drain very well and put on to a warm serving dish. Melt the butter and cook the breadcrumbs until just golden. Chop the egg and the crisply grilled bacon. Pour the butter and crumbs over the cauliflower and sprinkle with egg, bacon and parsley.

CELERIAC

Celeriac has the concentrated flavour of celery, and the texture of celery hearts. It is delicious both raw and cooked. Coarsely grated celeriac in French dressing or mayonnaise makes an excellent salad, but it may also be cooked in boiling water or stock until tender and served dressed with butter or white sauce. Celeriac also makes a good purée with cream and seasonings added.

CELERY

Celery is good raw and cooked. To prepare celery for eating raw with cheese, separate the stalks and wash them well, removing any blemishes. Leave a few of the young leaves on the stalks. Put the stalks into iced water containing a few ice cubes and leave in the refrigerator for two or three hours before serving. Drain well and serve very cold. Chopped raw celery is good in green salads, or mixed in seafood cocktails. Short lengths of celery may be used in casseroles, while long stalks or whole hearts can be braised in butter and stock to serve as a vegetable. It is worth drying some celery leaves like herbs, and using them to give a hint of celery flavour to dishes.

Celery Soup

1 head celery
1 large onion
50 g (2 oz) butter
1 carrot
1 large potato
1 teaspoon brown sugar
salt and pepper

250 ml (½ pint) chicken stock
500 ml (1 pint) milk

Clean the celery and cut into small pieces. Chop the onion. Melt the butter, add the celery and onion, and stir over gentle heat for 4 minutes. Add diced carrot and potato and cook for 2 minutes. Add sugar, salt and pepper, and 250 ml (½ pint) water and simmer until the vegetables are tender. Put through a sieve, return the purée to the pan with the stock and milk and simmer for 10 minutes.

CHICORY

Chicory may be eaten raw or cooked. The heads should be used when the tips are pale yellow and white. To serve as a salad, remove the outer leaves and rinse the heads in cold water. Use individual leaves, or cut across into circular slices, but use immediately after cutting, as chicory discolours quickly. Chicory should never be boiled to serve as a vegetable, but is best braised with a little lemon juice, salt and pepper, butter and a few spoonfuls or stock. Serve with white sauce or cheese sauce.

Chicory and Ham Rolls

8 chicory heads
8 thin slices cooked ham
50 g (2 oz) grated Cheddar cheese
500 ml (1 pint) white sauce
salt and pepper
25 g (1 oz) fresh breadcrumbs
25 g (1 oz) butter

Cook the chicory in a little water with a squeeze of lemon juice for 15 minutes, and drain very thoroughly. Wrap each head in a slice of ham and put in a shallow ovenware dish. Mix the cheese with the white sauce, season and pour over chicory. Sprinkle with breadcrumbs and dot with the butter. Bake at 190°C (375°F)/Gas 5 for 30 minutes.

COURGETTES see Marrow.

CUCUMBER

The cucumber is an attractive salad vegetable (see Chapter 5) but it may also be cooked. Small cucumbers may be cooked in the same way as courgettes (see page 10), and are good stuffed with a creamy ham and onion stuffing topped with cheese and baked until tender. They may also be cubed, poached and served in white sauce flavoured with dill.

8

ENDIVE

Endive, which is a species of chicory with curled leaves, makes a refreshing salad but it may also be cooked. Like spinach, it goes particularly well with cheese, and can be substituted in many spinach recipes. Both raw and cooked, endive has a slight bitterness.

Braised Endive

1 bunch endive
375 ml (¾ pint) beef stock
salt and pepper
25 g (1 oz) grated Parmesan cheese

Wash and drain the endive. Tear it into large pieces and cook in boiling salted water for 8 minutes. Drain well and arrange in a shallow ovenware dish. Pour on the beef stock and season well. Bake at 180°C (350°F)/Gas 4 for 20 minutes and sprinkle with cheese before serving.

LEEKS

For full details, see Chapter 3.

LETTUCE

Of course, lettuce makes good salads, but it also makes a number of good cooked dishes. This is useful for dealing with a glut as it cannot be frozen. Lettuce can be braised as a vegetable, or cooked with fresh green peas. Lettuce soups are good either hot or cold, made by cooking shredded lettuce with a little bacon fat or butter, then simmering in chicken stock with a few herbs and a little onion.

Braised Lettuce

4 small heads of lettuce
1 tablespoon olive oil
15 g (½ oz) butter
1 small onion
1 bacon rasher
4 tomatoes
1 tablespoon chopped parsley
1 teaspoon sugar
salt and pepper
pinch ground nutmeg

Wash the lettuces and keep them whole. Put into boiling salted water, bring to the boil again, take out the lettuces and drain them well. Heat oil and butter and add the chopped onion and bacon. Stir until soft and golden. Peel the tomatoes, remove the pips, and cut the flesh into pieces. Add to the onions and stir for 5 minutes. Put in the lettuce, parsley, sugar and seasonings, cover tightly and simmer for 30 minutes.

MARROWS AND COURGETTES

Marrows and small courgettes need careful cooking to keep their delicate flavour and texture. Marrow flesh is best steamed rather than boiled before serving with plenty of melted butter, or with white or cheese sauce. Courgettes should be eaten when young and small, with tender skins which are also eaten. They may be split lengthwise and baked with a stuffing of meat or cheese, served with cheese or tomato sauce. As a plain vegetable, they are best cut into 2·5-cm (1-in) slices with the skins on, and lightly fried in oil until golden.

Stuffed Marrow

1 large marrow
450 g (1 lb) cooked beef or lamb
50 g (2 oz) bacon
25 g (1 oz) plain flour
salt and pepper
50 g (2 oz) fresh breadcrumbs
1 teaspoon chopped parsley
2 tomatoes
25 g (1 oz) dripping

Peel the marrow and cut in half lengthwise. Scoop out the seeds and the pulp. Mince the meat and the bacon and mix with the flour, seasoning, breadcrumbs and parsley. Skin the tomatoes, take out the pips, and chop the flesh. Mix with the meat and fill the marrow. Put in a greased ovenware dish with the dripping and bake at 180°C (350°F)/Gas 4 for 1 hour, basting well. Serve with gravy.

MUSHROOMS

Mushrooms should be used very fresh, and should never be washed or peeled, but gently wiped to get rid of surface dirt. Only trim the ends of the stalks, because the stalk holds much of the mushroom's flavour. When cooking in butter, add a little oil to prevent the butter browning, and a squeeze of lemon juice, and cook just enough to make the mushrooms tender. Mushrooms are delicious raw in a dressing of oil and lemon juice, left for about 2 hours in the refrigerator to absorb the liquid.

Onions

For full details, see Chapter 3.

Parsnips

Parsnips are very good part-boiled, then roasted or fried, and they can be cooked around a joint like potatoes. Parsnips are also excellent mashed, either on their own or mixed with carrots or potatoes, with plenty of butter or a sprinkling of grated cheese.

Parsnip Balls

450 g (1 lb) parsnips
100 g (4 oz) butter
1 tablespoon milk
salt and pepper
1 egg, lightly beaten
100 g (4 oz) stale breadcrumbs

Cook the parsnips in boiling water. Drain, mash them and mix with the butter, milk and seasoning. Heat and stir until the mixture is thick. Cool and beat in a little of the egg to give a smooth mixture. Shape into 16 balls and roll these in the remaining egg, then dip into the breadcrumbs. Fry in hot fat until golden.

Peas

Peas are best eaten when young, tender and sweet, with a little mint and a pinch of sugar in the cooking water. Peas are also good cold, served as part of a salad.

Peas with Lettuce

25 g (1 oz) butter
12 spring onions
1 small lettuce
450 g (1 lb) shelled peas
salt and pepper
pinch ground nutmeg
1 teaspoon honey
tarragon, thyme and chervil

Melt the butter in a thick saucepan. Chop the onions and lettuce finely and put into the pan, topped with the peas. Season well with salt and pepper, nutmeg and honey. Chop the herbs and add about 1 tablespoon of them. Add 3 tablespoons water, cover tightly and cook very gently for 12 minutes. Serve very hot.

PEPPERS

Peppers go well with many other vegetables, particularly tomatoes and onions. They can be used raw in salads, or cooked in many ways. They may be stuffed and baked, particularly with rice in the stuffing, and a topping of fresh tomato sauce. Peppers must be carefully prepared to avoid the fiery little seeds. Cut away the stem and central core with a sharp knife, and remove all the soft membrane and tiny white seeds. Use whole or in halves for stuffing, or cut in strips or rings.

Green Peppers and Onions

> *2 tablespoons bacon fat*
> *2 green peppers*
> *1 onion*
> *¼ teaspoon salt*
> *pinch pepper*

Melt the fat and add sliced green peppers, sliced onion, and salt and pepper. Cover, and simmer for 10 minutes.

Peperonata

> *4 large red peppers*
> *6 large tomatoes*
> *50 g (2 oz) butter*
> *2 tablespoons olive oil*
> *1 onion*
> *salt*
> *1 garlic clove*
> *fresh basil*

Halve the peppers, remove the seeds and cut the flesh in strips. Skin and chop tomatoes. Melt the butter and olive oil together, and add the sliced onion. Soften the onion, add the peppers and simmer, covered, for 15 minutes. Add the tomatoes, salt and mashed garlic clove, and cook until the tomatoes and peppers are soft and the oil is absorbed, leaving a fairly dry mixture. Sprinkle on a little fresh basil. This dish can be eaten hot or cold, and reheats well.

Potatoes deserve careful cooking as a delicious vegetable. New potatoes are good cooked with mint, then drained and tossed in butter. A garnish of dill or chopped parsley helps to give them a special flavour. Older potatoes are good chipped or roasted (boil potatoes for 5 minutes before roasting for the best results), or baked in their jackets. Jacket potatoes may be served with nothing more than butter and seasoning, but they can also be filled with cream cheese, grated Cheddar cheese, creamed fish or chicken, or crisply grilled bacon.

Potato Casserole

15 g ($\frac{1}{2}$ oz) butter
1 garlic clove
salt
675 g (1$\frac{1}{2}$ lb) potatoes
50 g (2 oz) Cheddar cheese
pepper
grated nutmeg
250 ml ($\frac{1}{2}$ pint) milk
1 egg

Butter an ovenware dish. Crush the garlic clove with salt and spread this on the bottom of the dish. Peel and slice the potatoes very thinly, and put them in rows in the dish, sprinkling each layer with grated cheese, salt and pepper, and nutmeg. Bring the milk to the boil, beat with the egg, and pour on to the potatoes. Bake at 190°C (375°F)/Gas 5 for 1 hour. To avoid drying out, the dish can be placed in a tin of hot water while cooking.

Cottage Potato Bake

900 g (2 lb) potatoes
75 g (3 oz) butter
salt and pepper

Peel the potatoes and slice them thinly. In a large baking dish arrange one-third of the potatoes. Dot with butter and sprinkle with salt and pepper. Repeat with two more layers. Cover with foil and bake at 220°C (425°F)/Gas 7 for 40 minutes. Uncover for the last 10 minutes to brown the top layer of potatoes.

PUMPKINS

Pumpkins may be used for savoury and sweet dishes. It is better to steam or fry the flesh, rather than cooking it in water. Pumpkin flesh may be steamed until tender, then mashed or blended with some chicken stock and milk to the consistency of cream, and reheated to serve as soup. Salt and pepper are the usual seasoning, but some people like the addition of a pinch of ginger and a little brown sugar.

Pumpkin Pie

225 g (8 oz) shortcrust pastry
350 g (12 oz) steamed pumpkin purée
4 eggs, separated
225 g (8 oz) sugar
$\frac{1}{2}$ teaspoon ground cinnamon
$\frac{1}{4}$ teaspoon ground allspice
$\frac{1}{4}$ teaspoon ground ginger
15 g ($\frac{1}{2}$ oz) plain flour
3 tablespoons melted butter
125 ml ($\frac{1}{4}$ pint) single cream

Line a flan ring or pie plate with the pastry. Prick the pastry, cover with foil and baking beans and bake at 200°C (400°F)/Gas 6 for 20 minutes. Remove the foil and beans.

Mix the pumpkin with the beaten egg yolks, sugar, spices, flour, butter and cream. Beat the egg whites and a pinch of salt to soft peaks and fold into the mixture. Pour into the pastry case and bake at 160°C (325°F)/Gas 3 for 50 minutes. A little dried fruit or some nuts may be added if liked.

Spinach

Spinach needs to be very well washed in two or three waters, then shaken dry and cooked in a covered pan with a knob of butter and no extra water. The spinach needs frequent shaking or stirring so that it does not stick to the pan, and it will cook very quickly and reduce in bulk. It makes a good vegetable served on the leaf stems and dressed with butter, but the stems may be removed before cooking, and the spinach then finely chopped or made into purée. It may also be folded into white sauce to make a very creamy purée. Spinach goes particularly well with cheese and egg dishes.

Swedes

Swedes have a slightly sweeter flavour than turnips, and are particularly good with poultry. They are at their best cooked and made into a purée with plenty of seasoning and butter or single cream. Swedes blend well with potatoes in a purée, and any leftover mixture can be formed into flat cakes and fried to serve at a later meal. Turnip recipes may be used for swedes.

SWEETCORN

Sweetcorn must be prepared immediately for cooking after cutting because at room temperature the sugar in the corn quickly becomes starch and the calorie and carbohydrate values increase rapidly. This also happens as soon as the husks are removed, so do not take these off until ready to cook the corn-cobs. The perfect cob for cooking should have plump, tender kernels, full of milk, and surrounded by soft 'silk'. If you prefer to cook the kernels off the cob, scrape them off with a sharp-pointed knife. Cobs may be steamed over boiling water for 15 minutes, or cooked in boiling water for just 5 minutes with a pinch of sugar and a squeeze of lemon juice. They can also be left in their husks, with the 'silk' removed and a knob of butter inserted, and roasted in the oven at 180°C (350°F)/Gas 4 for 35 minutes. Corn should never be salted before cooking as this makes it tough.

Corn Fritters

100 g (4 oz) plain flour
pinch salt
2 eggs, separated
15 g (½ oz) sugar
50 g (2 oz) melted butter
50 ml (2 fl oz) milk
225 g (8 oz) cooked corn kernels

Mix the flour and salt and add the egg yolks, sugar, butter and milk to make a firm batter. Add the corn kernels. Whisk egg whites stiffly and fold in. Drop spoonfuls into deep hot fat or oil and fry until golden brown. Drain well and serve with chicken or bacon.

TOMATOES

Tomatoes are delicious hot or cold (for salad uses, see Chapter 5). In cooking, the tomato is used almost as widely as the onion to flavour hundreds of dishes. Tomatoes go well with meat, fish, eggs and cheese, partner rice and pasta, and are invaluable for soups and sauces. With a filling of chopped meat or fish, breadcrumbs and seasoning they can be baked in a little stock for a good main meal. Tomatoes can be grilled, fried or baked to accompany dishes, and benefit from a good sprinkling of herbs. Green tomatoes which are just beginning to turn colour may also be grilled or fried, and both green and red tomatoes make excellent chutney.

Fresh Tomato Soup

450 g (1 lb) tomatoes

500 ml (1 pint) stock
1 small onion
1 bayleaf
sprig parsley
sprig thyme
40 g (1½ oz) butter
40 g (1½ oz) plain flour
125 ml (¼ pint) milk
1 teaspoon sugar
salt and pepper

Put the tomatoes, stock, chopped onion and herbs into a saucepan and simmer for 1 hour. Put through a fine sieve. Melt the butter, work in the flour, and gradually add the tomato purée. Stir over gentle heat until the mixture comes to the boil. Stir in the milk, sugar, salt and pepper, and reheat gently. Serve with a garnish of fried or toasted bread cubes.

TURNIPS

Only small, young, mild turnips are worth eating, lightly cooked in water, and dressed with butter and seasoning. Turnip purée is particularly good with rich fat meats like duck, pork, ham and sausages. Turnips may be mixed with small onions to serve with roast meat, and they may be cooked in beef stock. Part-boiled turnips may be finished off around a roasting joint, basted with the meat juices occasionally.

Beans

With careful planning, it is possible to have home-grown beans right through the year. Runner, French and broad beans freeze really well of course, and runner beans may be salted. In addition, however, many beans can be grown for drying, providing a splendid variety of meals all year round. Many of these beans are dual-purpose, being excellent to eat when young and fresh, but equally good when dried and used during the winter months. Dried beans have always been recognised as a rich source of protein, and in many countries are used as substitutes for meat and fish.

Protein is composed of 22 amino acids. The human body is unable to manufacture eight of these, and they have to be obtained by eating protein-rich food. Soybeans and sprouted seeds (see Chapter 4) are exceptionally high in these eight vital amino acids. It is important, however, to obtain one's daily quota of protein from two or more foods which complete each other's amino acid levels; for instance, soybeans and green vegetables can together provide all the daily protein allowance, leaving at least a third of the daily calorie allowance for other foods. All types of dried beans contain protein, calcium, and vitamin B, and it is worth growing a wide variety to give differences of flavour, colour and shape to salads, casseroles and soups. Look out for small white haricot beans and navy beans, red or brown kidney beans, the delicate green flageolet, and soybeans. Adzuki and mung beans are mainly used for their sprouts (see Chapter 4).

17

Dried Beans

Beans seem to dry best if left on the plants in hot dry weather. When the shells are dry and papery, the beans can be removed, rubbed clean, and stored. If the autumn becomes wet, it is better to uproot the plants and hang them in an airy shed until the pods are crisp before shelling and storing the beans. The beans must be kept dry, preferably in a tightly sealed, moisture-proof storage jar or container. They should be kept in a cool place at a constant temperature, and they will keep in good condition for a year.

To use the beans, they must be soaked in cold water. It is generally recommended that they should be soaked overnight, although some experts say that 3–6 hours are enough because the beans may start to ferment and become slightly toxic. If you need the beans in a hurry, cover them with cold water, bring to the boil and simmer for an hour.

The most important thing to remember about cooking dried beans is never to salt them while cooking or they will be hard. For serving however, they do need plenty of seasoning with sea salt and freshly ground pepper. They go particularly well with olive oil, pork fat or rich poultry fat, and are a marvellous accompaniment to rich meats and to ham or bacon. All dried beans are good served as a vegetable with a dressing of butter, seasoning and herbs, and cold beans make excellent salads with a French dressing. The recipes in this chapter specify the best beans to use, but different kinds may be used, individually or in a mixture.

Broad Beans

Like most vegetables, these are best cooked when small and young. Many people actually like to eat the young pods as well. Very young beans may be served in their skins, but broad beans are more delicious if their thin skins are slipped off before serving. They are good tossed in butter or a little bacon fat, and they are particularly flavourful served with parsley sauce. Parsley, chives and savory are complementary herbs.

French Beans (Haricot verts)

Use dwarf beans while they are young and pencil-slim, and cook them whole, but if they have become a little large, cut them into chunks. Dress them with butter and seasoning, and add a little grated onion or crushed garlic if liked. Mix beans with mushrooms cooked in butter, or with peas, young carrots and sweetcorn kernels, or use them cold in salads with tomatoes.

It is sad that runner beans are traditionally shredded because they then lose so much flavour and texture. It is better to cook very young runner beans whole, or to slit them in half lengthwise, or to cut them in chunks. Season well and dress with butter to serve as a vegetable, which goes particularly well with chicken and roast or grilled meats.

Bean Salads

All kinds of beans make excellent salads which can be prepared from left-over vegetables or from some freshly-cooked ones.

French Bean Salad Mix cooked French beans in French dressing with sliced tomatoes, and garnish with a little cress and some hard-boiled egg yolk. Alternatively, mix beans with French dressing, and garnish with anchovy fillets and finely chopped hard-boiled eggs.

Italian Salad Use cooked French or haricot beans and mix with French dressing, a little finely chopped onion and pieces of drained canned tuna.

Bean Pod Salad Use very young broad bean pods when no more than 5 cm (2 in) long and cook in boiling salted water. Cool and mix with French dressing, a little chopped onion and parsley. This is particularly good served with cold ham.

Bean and Pepper Salad Mix cooked small whole French beans with sliced raw green peppers and tomatoes. Dress with French dressing and serve with a garnish of chopped hard-boiled eggs.

Bean and Ham Salad Mix some cooked green flageolet beans with French dressing and a clove of crushed garlic. Add a layer of cooked ham, cut in strips, and some slices of hard-boiled eggs.

Broad Bean Salad

450 g (1 lb) shelled broad beans
1 teaspoon made mustard
1 teaspoon paprika
1 garlic clove
salt and pepper
1 tablespoon chopped parsley
1 tablespoon wine vinegar
3 tablespoons olive oil

Cook the beans in boiling water until tender and slip them from their outer skins while still hot. In a serving bowl, mix the mustard, paprika, crushed garlic, salt and pepper, parsley, vinegar and oil. Add the beans, and toss them in the dressing just before serving.

Red Bean Salad

450 g (1 lb) red kidney beans
1 garlic clove
1 tablespoon wine vinegar
3 tablespoons olive oil
large pinch mustard powder
pinch tarragon
salt and pepper
1 small onion
3 tomatoes

Rinse the beans, cover them with water, bring to the boil and boil for two minutes. Take off the heat and leave the beans in the water for 1 hour. Bring back to the boil and simmer for an hour until tender but not broken. Drain the beans thoroughly. Mix the crushed garlic, vinegar, oil, mustard, tarragon, salt and pepper very thoroughly. Pour over the hot beans and leave them to cool. Chop the onion very finely. Peel the tomatoes, take out the seeds and chop the flesh. Mix the onions and tomatoes with the beans, chill and serve.

Greek Bean Salad

225 g (8 oz) dried haricot beans
125 ml (¼ pint) olive oil
1 medium-sized onion
2 garlic cloves
1 bayleaf
pinch thyme
1 dessertspoon tomato purée
salt and pepper
juice of 1 lemon
2 tablespoons chopped parsley

Soak the beans in water overnight and drain. Heat the oil in a saucepan. Chop the onion and add to the oil and cook until soft and golden. Add the beans, crushed garlic cloves, bayleaf, thyme and tomato purée and cook gently for 10 minutes. Add enough boiling water to cover the beans by 2·5 cm (1 in) and simmer for about 2 hours until the beans are tender and the water has just been absorbed. Season well with salt and pepper, and add the lemon juice. Cool completely and stir in the parsley.

Some raw onion rings may be added, or some small pieces of lamb which have been cooked in the oil and simmered for 1 hour with the beans.

Jacket Beans

675 g (1½ lb) young broad beans in pods
salt and pepper
squeeze of lemon juice
25 g (1 oz) butter
3 tablespoons double cream
1 tablespoon chopped parsley

Use very young beans with tender pods. Wash the pods well, top and tail them, and cook in unsalted boiling water for 15 minutes. Drain thoroughly. Season with salt and pepper and lemon juice and toss in the butter, cream and parsley. Heat very gently and serve.

French Beans with Cream

675 g (1½ lb) French beans
2 bacon rashers
50 g (2 oz) onion
50 g (2 oz) green pepper
125 ml (¼ pint) water
salt and pepper
3 tablespoons single cream

Remove any strings from the beans and leave them whole (they should be young and about the thickness of a bootlace). Chop the bacon and heat gently until the fat runs. Add the chopped onion and pepper and stir over a low heat for 5 minutes. Add the beans and water and cover tightly. Simmer for 15 minutes until the beans are tender and the water absorbed. Season with salt and pepper, stir in the cream and serve hot.

Runner Beans and Mushrooms

450 g (1 lb) runner beans
1 small onion
1 small green pepper
2 bacon rashers
225 g (8 oz) mushrooms
75 g (3 oz) butter
salt and pepper

pinch nutmeg
4 tablespoons single cream
50 g (2 oz) grated Cheddar cheese

Remove tips from beans and cut in chunks. Chop the onion, pepper and bacon in small pieces. Put the bacon into a thick pan and heat until the fat runs. Add the onion and pepper and continue cooking until soft and golden. Add the beans and 125 ml ($\frac{1}{4}$ pint) water, cover and cook gently for 15 minutes until the beans are tender. Wipe the mushrooms without peeling them, and cook them in the butter for 5 minutes. Drain the cooking liquid from the beans. Mix the beans with the mushrooms, season with salt, pepper and nutmeg, and stir in the cream. Put into an ovenware dish, sprinkle with cheese and grill under a medium heat until the top is golden and bubbling.

Broad Bean Soup

675 g (1$\frac{1}{2}$ lb) shelled broad beans
2 bacon rashers
1 small onion
25 g (1 oz) butter
25 g (1 oz) plain flour
salt and pepper
1 teaspoon chopped parsley

Cook the beans in 1·5 litres (3 pints) water for 10 minutes and then drain. Keep the cooking liquid for the soup. Slip the thin skins off the beans. Cut the bacon and onion into small pieces and cook in the butter until soft and golden. Work in the flour and then gradually add the reserved cooking liquid. Stir over a gentle heat until the mixture is smooth, and then add the cooked beans. Put into an electric blender and blend until smooth, or press through a sieve. Season with salt and pepper, reheat and serve garnished with parsley.

Navy Soup

175 g (6 oz) dried haricot beans
2 carrots
1 stick celery
225 g (8 oz) tomato purée
1 medium-sized onion
3 garlic cloves
2 tablespoons chopped parsley
4 tablespoons olive or salad oil
salt and pepper
1 teaspoon lemon juice

The ideal beans for this soup are the small *Comtesse de Chambord*. Soak the beans in water overnight. Next day, drain and boil in fresh water for 30 minutes. Chop the carrots and celery. Add all the ingredients to the beans except the salt, pepper and lemon juice, and simmer for 1½ hours, adding a little more water if necessary. Remove from the heat and leave to stand for 1 hour. Reheat just to boiling point, and season with salt, pepper and lemon juice. Serve with a garnish of fried or toasted bread cubes.

Chili Con Carne

225 g (8 oz) dried haricot or red kidney beans
1 large onion
1 garlic clove
50 g (2 oz) butter
450 g (1 lb) raw minced beef
1 teaspoon chilli powder
25 g (1 oz) tomato purée

Soak the beans overnight, then drain them well and cover with fresh water. Cook for at least 1 hour until tender but not broken and drain them. Chop the onion and garlic and cook in the butter until soft and golden. Stir in the meat and cook until well-browned, stirring well all the time so that the pieces of meat are separate and not lumpy. Stir in the chilli powder, then the beans and tomato juice. Cover and leave on a low heat for 30 minutes, adding a little water if necessary so that the sauce is creamy. The chilli powder is very hot, so if you are not used to it, only put in a little at first and taste the mixture before adding the rest.

Lamb and Bean Casserole

100 g (4 oz) red kidney beans
3 tablespoons oil
675 g (1½ lb) shoulder lamb, cut in cubes
2 leeks
1 tablespoon chopped parsley
juice of 1 lemon
1 teaspoon dill leaves
2 teaspoons turmeric powder
1 teaspoon chopped mint
salt and pepper

Soak the beans overnight and then drain them. Cover with fresh water and boil for 1 hour. Drain and keep the liquid for stock. Heat the oil and fry the lamb cubes on all sides. Drain the lamb, reserving the oil, and put into a casserole. Cut the leeks into thin slices and fry in the oil until golden. Add to the casserole with the parsley, lemon juice, dill, turmeric and mint. Season with salt and pepper and pour on 500 ml (1 pint) of the reserved bean stock. Cover and cook gently for 1 hour. Add the beans and continue cooking for 20 minutes.

Haricot Beef Casserole

100 g (4 oz) dried haricot beans
1 large onion
2 tablespoons oil
450 g (1 lb) shin beef
250 ml (½ pint) tomato juice
500 ml (1 pint) water
225 g (8 oz) tomato purée

Soak the beans overnight, and drain. Peel and chop the onion and fry in the oil until lightly golden. Cut the beef in cubes and add to the oil, frying until sealed on all sides. Put the onions and beef into a casserole with the beans and cover with the tomato juice, water and tomato purée. Cover and bake at 180°C (350°F)/Gas 4 for 3 hours. Reduce heat to 150°C (300°F)/Gas 2 for 1 hour. Red kidney beans are good in this dish, too.

Pork and Beans

350 g (12 oz) dried haricot or red kidney beans
2 large onions
2 carrots
2 cloves
salt and pepper
1 tablespoon oil
225 g (8 oz) lean pork
25 g (1 oz) black treacle
6 bacon rashers
6 pork sausages
225 g (8 oz) garlic sausage
125 ml (¼ pint) red wine

Soak the beans in water overnight. Drain and put them into a pan with 750 ml (1½ pints) water, the chopped onions and carrots, cloves, salt and pepper. Cover and simmer for 1½ hours.

Heat the oil and brown cubes of pork on all sides. Drain off the oil and put into the bottom of a large casserole. Put in half the beans, then the pork and the remaining beans. Add the black treacle and top with the bacon rashers. Cover and bake at 150°C (300°F)/Gas 2 for 4 hours.

Grill the sausages and cut them into pieces. Cut the garlic sausage into cubes. Add the sausage and garlic sausage to the casserole with twine. Cover and cook for a further 30 minutes.

Farmhouse Beans

225 g (8 oz) dried butter or haricot beans
2 sticks celery
1 medium-sized onion
1 bayleaf
pinch bicarbonate of soda
40 g (1½ oz) butter
40 g (1½ oz) plain flour
375 ml (¾ pint) milk
50 g (2 oz) grated Cheddar cheese
salt and pepper
pinch ground nutmeg
2 tomatoes
1 tablespoon chopped parsley

Soak the beans overnight, and drain. Put them into a pan with fresh water, the chopped celery and onion, bayleaf and soda. Bring to the boil and simmer for 1 hour. Drain and discard the bayleaf. Make a white sauce by melting the butter and working in the flour. Cook for 3 minutes, then gradually stir in the milk and cook gently until the sauce is creamy. Remove from the heat and stir in the cheese, salt, pepper and nutmeg. Mix the beans and vegetables with the sauce and turn into an ovenware serving dish. Slice the tomatoes and arrange on top. Put under a medium-hot grill until the top is golden, garnish with chopped parsley and serve at once.

Buttered Red Beans

450 g (1 lb) dried red kidney beans
50 g (2 oz) butter
salt and pepper

Rinse the beans and cover them with water. Bring to the boil and boil for two minutes. Take off the heat and leave the beans in the water for 1 hour. Bring back to the boil and simmer for an hour until tender but not broken. Drain and toss the beans in butter, salt and pepper until the butter has melted. Serve as a vegetable with meat, poultry or fish.

Boston Baked Beans

450 g (1 lb) dried haricot beans
2 teaspoons mustard powder

1 teaspoon salt
1 teaspoon black pepper
50 g (2 oz) tomato purée
1 tablepsoon golden syrup
1 tablespoon black treacle
50 g (2 oz) dark soft brown sugar
2 large onions
225 g (8 oz) salt belly pork
1 tablespoon oil

Soak the beans overnight, and then drain. Mix the mustard, salt and pepper in an ovenware casserole. Add the beans, cover with water, and stir in the tomato purée, syrup, treacle and brown sugar. Peel and quarter the onions and add to the casserole. Cover and bake at 140°C (275°F)/Gas 1 for 8 hours, adding a little water if necessary so the beans do not become dry.

Soak the pork in cold water, and when the beans have been cooking for 6 hours, drain the meat and cut it into 2·5-cm (1-in) cubes. Brown them quickly on all sides in the oil, and add to the casserole for the remaining 2 hours.

Honey-baked Beans

225 g (8 oz) dried haricot beans
3 medium-sized tomatoes
1 medium-sized onion
75 g (3 oz) honey
1 teaspoon French mustard
3 bacon rashers
pinch bicarbonate of soda
2 tablespoons olive oil

Soak the beans overnight and then simmer in fresh water until tender but not broken. Drain and mix with the skinned tomatoes, cut in quarters. Add the chopped onion, honey, mustard, diced bacon and soda. Put into a well-greased casserole and pour on the olive oil. Cover and bake at 160°C (325°F)/Gas 3 for 3 hours. Serve with some home-made tomato sauce.

Soybean Loaf

250 g (9 oz) soybeans
1 chicken stock cube
pinch sage
1 teaspoon chopped onion
salt and pepper
1 teaspoon Worcestershire sauce

125 ml (¼ pint) tomato juice
1 stick celery
1 small green pepper
1 medium-sized carrot

Soak the beans overnight, drain and cook in fresh water for 1 hour. Drain and cool. Put into an electric blender with the stock cube, sage, onion, salt and pepper, Worcestershire sauce and tomato juice. Blend until smooth. Mix with finely chopped celery, pepper and carrot. Put into a casserole or loaf tin and bake at 200°C (400°F)/Gas 6 for 45 minutes. Serve hot or cold with tomato sauce.

Onions

The onion family has always been the cook's friend, adding subtle flavour to hundreds of dishes. Onions, leeks, shallots and garlic all have their special properties and individual flavours, but they also deserve recognition for their medicinal qualities. Traditionally onions are a stimulant to the digestion and an aid to sound sleep. In fact, the onion has high protein and mineral content and contains vitamins B, C and G. Because of the high oil and sugar content, the onion is also high in calories. A large onion retains heat at its centre and for this reason onions were used as homely remedies, being made into poultices and ear soothers. An onion syrup was a popular decongestant for children, helping to release the phlegm in their lungs.

Onions

Perfect onions should be firm and hard, with thin tight necks and crisp skin. They should not be used when sprouting, or if they have thick soft necks or spongy bulbs. Onions should be stored in a cool dry place, preferably strung up in the air. Old onions are stronger in flavour than new ones, but boiling reduces the strength of flavour, and the onion takes longer than most vegetables to cook. It is important not to add too much fat to onion dishes, as they contain plenty of their own oil.

Onions cause tears, but there are many remedies suggested for less troublesome peeling. Some people hold a knife or a crust of bread in their teeth; others peel the onion under cold running water. French experts peel the onion, leave it to stand for a few minutes, and then chop the flesh without tears.

To rid your hands of onion smells, wash them in cold water and salt, or wash them in cold water and rub them with freshly-chopped parsley, celery tops or lemon before washing with soap and cold water. For the breath, eat a little sugar, chew a coffee bean, sprig of parsley or a clove. Or drink a cup of strong black coffee or a glass of milk.

The onion is perfect in so many dishes. Onions can be served simply with grilled meat or sausages and boiled or mashed potatoes; they combine well with cheese for supper snacks, are essential to many meat pies and pasties, and are important in many sauces. Plenty of salt and freshly ground black pepper bring out onion flavour, and this is also improved by a pinch of mustard powder or a grating of nutmeg. A brown or white sauce with onions cooked in it makes the perfect accompaniment to both beef and lamb, and a herb and onion stuffing helps to counteract the richness of fat meats like duck and goose.

The same astringent quality is valuable in salads. A little finely chopped onion enhances tomato, beetroot and potato salads, and a combination of orange slices and onion rings is delicious with duck and game. If raw onion is considered indigestible, the salad onions should be sliced and covered with boiling water, then left to stand for 30 minutes. Then the rings should be drained, covered with ice cold water and left for 30 minutes to become crisp. These onion rings can then be used like raw onions.

Properly stored onions should keep for many months, but it is worth freezing some for a quick addition to dishes, and small ones of course make a popular pickle.

Onions in their Jackets

6 large onions
butter
salt and pepper

Take any loose outer skin from the onions, but leave as much skin as possible. Put the onions on a baking tin in the bottom of the oven in which a joint or casserole is cooking. Cook until the onions are tender (about 1 hour at moderate heat). Test them by inserting a skewer, which will go easily to the centre when the onions are done. Serve very hot with plenty of butter, salt and pepper.

Braised Onions

6 medium-sized onions
100 g (4 oz) dripping
250 ml (½ pint) stock
flour
salt and pepper
juice of ½ lemon

Peel the onions and put them into a heavy pan with the dripping. Cover tightly and cook gently until the onions are golden. Drain off the fat and cover the onions with stock. Simmer until they are soft but not broken. Thicken the liquid with a little flour and season with salt, pepper and lemon juice. A larger number of small onions may be cooked in the same way, but must be watched very carefully when they are cooking in the dripping so they do not over-brown. These onions are excellent with beef or lamb.

Glazed Onions

450 g (1 lb) small onions
50 g (2 oz) butter
1 tablespoon sugar

Peel the onions and cook them in salted water until almost soft. Drain well. Melt the butter in a pan, add the onions and sprinkle with sugar. Cover and simmer until the onions are golden brown and tender. Serve hot with beef, lamb or veal.

Golden Onion Rings

1 large onion
milk
salt and pepper
flour
1 egg yolk

Peel the onion and cut into 0·5-cm (¼-in) slices. Separate the slices into rings and soak in equal quantities of milk and water for 30 minutes. Drain the rings, season with salt and pepper and coat with flour. Beat the egg yolk with a little milk and dip the onion rings in the mixture. Dip them again in flour and leave on a wire cake rack until they have dried a little. Fry in deep fat until crisp and golden. Use to garnish cheese or meat dishes.

Sage and Onion Stuffing

450 g (1 lb) onions

100 g (4 oz) soft white breadcrumbs
2 teaspoons finely chopped fresh sage
25 g (1 oz) butter
salt and pepper

Peel and chop the onions and simmer them in just enough water to cover for 10 minutes. Strain and keep the cooking water. Mix the onions with the crumbs, sage, butter and seasoning, and add just enough reserved water to bind the stuffing. Use for fat meats such as pork, duck and goose.

Onion Soup

675 g (1½ lb) onions
50 g (2 oz) butter
1·5 litres (3 pints) beef stock
salt and pepper
100 g (4 oz) grated cheese
4 slices of French bread

Peel the onions and slice them finely. Cook them gently in the butter until soft and golden. Add the stock and seasoning and bring to the boil. Reduce the heat and simmer for 25 minutes. Just before serving, put cheese on to slices of French bread, allowing one piece for each person. Toast until the cheese melts and put the slices into a tureen or individual bowls. Pour over the soup and serve very hot.

Stuffed Onions

4 large onions
225 g (8 oz) cooked minced beef or lamb
50 g (2 oz) fresh breadcrumbs
125 ml (¼ pint) brown gravy
1 teaspoon tomato purée
salt and pepper

Peel the onions and boil them until just tender. Take out the centres with a pointed knife and chop the flesh finely. Mix with the meat, crumbs (reserving a few for a light topping), gravy, purée and seasoning. Put this filling into the onions, and place them in an ovenware dish with a little dripping. Sprinkle a few breadcrumbs on top and bake at 200°C (400°F)/Gas 6 for 45 minutes. Serve with extra gravy.

Sage and Onion Tart

225 g (8 oz) shortcrust pastry
3 medium-sized onions

25 g (1 oz) butter
125 ml (¼ pint) creamy milk
1 egg
1 tablespoon fresh sage
1 teaspoon fresh parsley
100 g (4 oz) bacon
salt and pepper

Line a flan ring or pie plate with the pastry. Peel the onions, chop them finely, and toss in hot butter until soft and golden. Mix with the milk, beaten egg, finely chopped herbs, chopped bacon and seasoning. Pour into the pastry case. Bake at 200°C (400°F)/Gas 6 for 35 minutes. The herbs and bacon may be omitted but they give an excellent flavour to this simple tart. Some grated cheese may be added if liked.

A quick onion flan can be made by filling a ready-cooked pastry case with cooked onions in white sauce, and browning the top under a grill.

Pissaladière

275 g (10 oz) strong plain flour
salt
7 g (¼ oz) dried yeast
75-g (3-oz) tin anchovies
450 g (1 lb) onions
8 tablespoons olive oil
pepper
3 tomatoes
100 g (4 oz) black olives

Sift the flour into a warm bowl with a pinch of salt. Dissolve the yeast in 6 tablespoons warm water and leave until it is frothy (about 10 minutes). Stir the yeast mixture into the flour and work together until smooth, adding a little more warm water if necessary to make the dough stick together. Knead the dough until firm and smooth, put into an oiled bowl, cover with a damp cloth and leave in a warm place while preparing the other ingredients.

Soak the anchovies in a little water, changing the water several times. Peel the onions and slice them into thin rings. Heat 6 tablespoons oil and cook the onions over a low heat for about 40 minutes, stirring well and softening the onions almost to a purée, without colouring. Season with salt and freshly ground black pepper. Peel the tomatoes.

Roll out the dough into a large circle and put on a greased baking sheet, rolling the edges up to form a rim (if preferred, the dough can be put into a flan ring). Prick the dough well with a fork. Spread the bottom with the onions and top with thin slices of tomato, the drained anchovy fillets and olives arranged in a pattern. Sprinkle with the remaining oil and bake at 200°C (400°F)/Gas 6 for 25 minutes.

This is a popular Provençal dish and may be made without the tomatoes if preferred. Instead of using a bread dough, the base can be made from ordinary scone mixture. The onion and anchovy mixture can also be used in a pastry case, or used to top slices of fried bread for a quick snack.

SHALLOTS

Shallots, which have a mild flavour, are not used enough in the British kitchen, although they are essential to classic French cooking. They are particularly important for such sauces as Béarnaise which need the light whiff of onion. Shallots are seldom used as a vegetable on their own, but are often pickled. They are delicious braised and served in a white or brown sauce. For general kitchen use, they are best left to dry after harvesting, and then hung in a small net bag in the kitchen, so that they can easily be used when a slight taste of onion is needed.

Sauce Bordelaise (for steak)

1 tablespoon finely chopped shallot
1 large wineglass dry red wine
1 teaspoon crushed peppercorns
1 sprig thyme
1 wineglass beef stock
1 tablespoon butter
1 teaspoon plain flour
salt

Cook the shallot in a little extra butter until golden. Add the red wine, peppercorns and thyme and cook until the liquid has two-thirds evaporated. Add the beef stock and the butter and flour mixed together and cook until thick. Season with salt and put the sauce through a fine sieve. If acid-tasting, add a little more butter just before serving. A little lemon juice and cubed cooked bone marrow is sometimes added.

Sauce Béarnaise (for beef and lamb)

1 tablespoon chopped shallot
½ teaspoon chopped tarragon
5 tablespoons vinegar
3 egg yolks
250 g (9 oz) butter

pinch chervil
salt and pepper

Chop the shallot very finely and put it into a saucepan with the tarragon and vinegar. Cook until all the liquid has evaporated. Take from the heat and add 3 tablespoons cold water. Add the egg yolks and beat well with a whisk. Put back on a low heat and stir until the yolks thicken, being careful that the eggs do not cook. Melt the butter in a separate container and add to the egg mixture drop by drop at first, then a little more at a time. Don't use the bottom of the butter, which will spoil the consistency of the sauce. Stir constantly while the butter is added, and then season with chervil, salt and pepper. Serve warm, but not hot.

Poultry Flavouring (for roast chicken)

2 tablespoons chopped parsley
1 tablespoon chopped shallot
a little rosemary
1 teaspoon chives
1 tablespoon butter or olive oil

Chop the herbs very finely indeed and mix with the butter or oil. Push the mixture under the skin of a chicken's breast bone, rubbing it down the breast and over the sides without breaking the skin. This gives a subtle flavour and is excellent when the bird is left to become cold before slicing.

Leeks

Leeks have a deliciously mild flavour, and don't leave a smell on the breath, so they are invaluable in the kitchen when a light onion flavour is needed. They stand happily in the garden during winter months, but their delicacy is suitable for many summer dishes, so that it is worth freezing some of the crop for year-round use.

Leeks are excellent in soups and stews, and taste better if lightly tossed in butter before added to dishes. They should only be gently coloured and softened, and not cooked until brown. Lightly cooked leeks can also be used cold in salads, or a few rings of raw leek may be used in winter salads. A small quantity of leeks simmered in a little water or stock can be drained, chopped finely and added to a white or cheese sauce to serve over cauliflower or broccoli. Leeks cooked in butter and chopped finely are excellent added to a hot potato salad, or make an easy filling for omelettes. The delicate flavour blends well with chicken, ham and bacon, and is good with cheese and eggs, and leeks are also good with Jerusalem artichokes and potatoes in soups or pies.

34

It is very important to clean leeks properly as light earth gets between the layers and can be difficult to remove. Trim off the roots, and then the green tops to within 2·5 cm (1 in) of the white bulb. Large leeks may be split lengthwise before cooking, or they may be cut in rings before simmering in water or stock, or softening in butter.

Leek Salad

8 medium-sized leeks
6 tablespoons olive oil
3 tablespoons tarragon vinegar
1 garlic clove
salt
freshly ground black pepper
½ teaspoon made mustard

Remove the roots and tops from the leeks, cutting about 2·5 cm (1 in) above the white part. Wash carefully and cut into slices about 1 cm (½ in) thick. Cook in boiling salted water for 7 minutes until just tender. Drain well and rinse in cold water. Put the oil, vinegar, crushed garlic, salt, pepper and mustard into a bowl and work them together until well blended. Pour over the leeks and chill before serving.

This is also good made with thinnings from the leek bed when they are about the size of spring onions, in which case the leeks can be left whole.

Leek Soup

3 medium-sized leeks
450 g (1 lb) potatoes
25 g (1 oz) butter
750 ml (1¼ pints) chicken stock
salt and pepper
chives

Remove roots and green leaves from leeks and wash the leeks very well. Cut into 1-cm (½-in) rings. Peel the potatoes and cut into 2·5-cm (1-in) dice. Melt the butter in a thick saucepan and toss the leeks over a low heat until they are just soft but not coloured. Add the potatoes and chicken stock and simmer until the potatoes are cooked but not broken up. Serve very hot, well-seasoned and with a sprinkling of finely chopped chives.

This soup can be given many different treatments. For a rough country soup, add some small dice of cooked chicken (or turkey) and serve as above. Toasted or fried bread cubes can be sprinkled on top, and chopped parsley can be added to the garnish. A little milk or cream can also be stirred in just before serving. The soup can also be sieved or liquidised and milk added during reheating. This purée may be sieved, chilled and served with cream as the classic Vichyssoise.

Leek Pudding

2 large leeks
100 g (4 oz) plain flour
½ teaspoon baking powder
¼ teaspoon salt
40 g (1½ oz) shredded suet

Remove the roots and tops from the leeks, cutting about 2·5 cm (1 in) above the white part. Cut each leek in half lengthwise and wash very thoroughly, then chop the halves into small pieces. Sift the flour, baking powder and salt together and stir in the shredded suet. Add the leek pieces and enough cold water to make a fairly stiff consistency, mixing very lightly. Turn into a greased basin, cover, and steam for 2½ hours. Serve with gravy or cheese sauce, or cut in slices to eat with meat or chicken.

Devon Leek Pie

225 g (8 oz) shortcrust pastry
6 large leeks
250 ml (½ pint) milk
salt and pepper
75 ml (3 fl oz) single cream

Roll out the pastry to make a lid for a pie dish. Remove the roots and tops from the leeks, cutting about 2·5 cm (1 in) above the white part. Wash very well and cut into 2·5-cm (1-in) pieces. Put the leeks in a pan together with the milk, salt, and pepper and simmer gently until they are tender. Turn the mixture into the pie dish, stir in the cream and cover with pastry. Bake at 200°C (400°F)/Gas 6 for 30 minutes and serve with cold meat.

Leek Flan

Many people enjoy an open leek flan. First line a flan ring or pie dish with shortcrust pastry. Cut up 6 large leeks and put them into the pastry case (they taste best if they are first slightly softened in butter). Season well and pour on 250 ml (½ pint) creamy milk beaten with 2 eggs. Bake at 200°C (400°F)/Gas 6 for 35–40 minutes until golden. A little grated cheese added to the liquid will make this a complete supper dish served on its own.

GARLIC

Of the onion family, garlic has the strongest flavour. It lingers on the breath, and the smell can be exuded by the pores of the skin. But garlic gives such a special strong warm flavour to dishes that many people are ready to risk the after-effects. In fact, the lingering after-taste and smell can be dispersed by chewing fresh parsley or a coffee bean.

Almost magical powers are attributed to garlic, which was eaten by the ancient Egyptians and was used in the ceremonial taking of oaths. Ulysses was supposed to have escaped from the enchantress Circe through the virtues of garlic. It has certain antiseptic qualities, and is recommended particularly for warding off colds and aiding chest congestion. It is supposed to clear the complexion if eaten constantly for a few days, has been used as a treatment for leprosy, and during the First World War the raw juice was used to prevent wounds turning septic.

Those who like the flavour will appreciate the fact that garlic aids digestion, and is said to keep the stomach lining in good condition. If only a delicate flavour is liked, a cut clove can be rubbed around a casserole or salad bowl. A better flavour for salads is achieved by rubbing stale bread with cut garlic, then dicing the bread, sprinkling it with olive oil, and tossing the cubes with the salad dressing just before serving the salad. If liked, the dice may be fried in olive oil before they are added to the dressing.

Garlic should not be kept too long in a dry place or it will shrivel. The flavour can be kept for salads if a few crushed cloves are added to a bottle of wine vinegar. The individual cloves should be skinned, then finely chopped with a sharp knife. They can then be easily crushed by sprinkling them with a little coarse salt and exerting a heavy pressure on the cloves with a flat-bladed knife. Allow for the addition of this extra salt when making up a recipe.

Garlic Bread

1 French loaf
75 g (3 oz) butter
3 garlic cloves

Cut the French loaf through in 5-cm (2-in) diagonal chunks without cutting right to the bottom. Cream the butter and add crushed garlic cloves. Mix well and spread between slices of bread. Wrap bread in foil and put into a hot oven for 15 minutes until the bread is crisp and the butter has melted and soaked into the crumb. Eat hot with barbecued meat or fish, or cold meals. For a party, loaves of bread may be prepared in advance and heated through just before serving.

Garlic Sauce (Aioli)

3 garlic cloves
2 egg yolks
salt and pepper
1 teaspoon mustard powder
170 ml ($\frac{1}{3}$ pint) olive oil
1 teaspoon lemon juice

Crush the garlic cloves and then work in the egg yolks, salt, pepper and mustard. Mix well together and gradually add the olive oil drop by drop, stirring with a wooden spoon or wire whisk. When all the oil has been incorporated and the mixture is thick, add the lemon juice.

This classic Provençal sauce sometimes has a few breadcrumbs added, but is in effect garlic mayonnaise. It is good served with fish, boiled beef, and plainly cooked vegetables, particularly beans, onions, globe artichokes and fennel.

Spring Onions

Spring onions, sometimes known by the old name of 'scallions', are the most widely grown of all the onion family. They grow quickly and are hardy, and are available most of the year except during the coldest months. They are most often used raw in salads, but can be used as a substitute for leeks in summer recipes, although a large quantity is needed to make up the necessary bulk. The little white bulbs are delicious cooked with peas, or they can be used in savoury flans. Spring onions are very good if chopped and made into brown bread sandwiches, and they blend particularly well with cream cheese.

Welsh Onions

These are a useful permanent source of 'spring onions' in the garden. The Welsh onion grows in clusters, like bunches of spring onions. Individual onions can be removed from the clump without damage to the plant.

Chives

The finely chopped stems of chives are useful for giving a light onion flavour to all sorts of dishes, but the bulbs are not used. The stems are best cut finely with scissors, and can be used to flavour creamed potatoes, cottage or cream cheese, mayonnaise and salad dressings, and soups. Chives are very good in egg dishes. Try them in scrambled eggs, in sandwiches made with hard-boiled eggs and mayonnaise, and mixed with a

38

little chopped crisp bacon under baked eggs.

Chives form part of the classic *fines herbes* when mixed with parsley, tarragon and chervil, and are particularly used in this mixture in omelettes. Either on their own, or with other herbs, they are essential to a good beetroot salad, to tomato salad, and to hot or cold potato salad.

Chive Butter

butter
chopped chives

Cream the butter and mix with finely chopped chives in the proportion of two parts butter to one part chives. Form into a cylinder and wrap in foil or greaseproof paper. Chill before using and cut into circles for serving. Use pieces of chive butter on grilled meat or fish, on freshly cooked carrots and beans, and on oven-baked jacket potatoes.

Sprouting Seeds

Anyone who has ever grown a delicious snack of mustard and cress on a piece of wet flannel, or a bean in a jam jar, will know how easy it is to garden without earth, and indeed without space. Today, the sprouts of a wide variety of seeds, cereals and beans can be grown in a few days to provide essential protein and vitamins. Sprouts are easily digested, because in the sprouting process starches are converted to simple sugars, and each kind of sprout contains vitamins and varying quantities of protein (see individual listings for food values).

The equipment for sprouting seeds is very simple. There are a number of methods, but sprouting in a jam jar is clean and easy, and this method is recommended. It is most important only to use seeds specially sold for sprouting as they must be free from chemicals, and certified as edible. For variety, sprouts can be grown from familiar foods such as brown rice and lentils, but often these will be cracked, broken or too old to sprout successfully.

Most sprouts are harvested when they are between 3–5 days old. As sprouts become older, they lose flavour and food value, and after 7–10 days they will be past their best. Sprouts will keep crisp for a week in the salad compartment of the refrigerator. To use the sprouts, rinse them well to get rid of any ungerminated or hard seeds. Sprouts may be eaten raw, in salads for instance, or lightly steamed, or simmered for 4 minutes. Sprouts should always be slightly 'crisp' to eat. They mix well with other vegetables such as beans or greens, and also go very well with eggs, fish, chicken and pork. Sprouts can be used in the stuffing of large tomatoes, peppers, aubergines or potatoes, giving a slightly crunchy texture, and they may also be included in scones, pancakes and fruit breads. One or two kinds of sprouts can be baked and ground to give added flavour to cakes. Another good use for these health-packed sprouts is in fruit, vegetable, or yoghurt drinks whipped up in an electric blender. The recipes given on pages 44–54 are for Alfalfa, Fenugreek, Adzuki Bean, Chinese (Mung) Bean and Triticale, which are available specially for sprouting. The other kinds of sprouts recommended may be substituted in recipes. *Two kinds of sprouts must not be eaten : tomato and potato.*

BASIC SPROUTING METHOD

Four level teaspoons of seed equals approximately 15 g ($\frac{1}{2}$ oz) seed. This will convert into 150–225 g (5–8 oz) food.

1. Take a thoroughly cleaned jam jar and cut a piece of muslin that will fit fully over the opening.

2. Put in 4 teaspoons seed and cover with the muslin lid, securing it with a small elastic band.

3. Fill with tepid water through the muslin and shake vigorously to clean the seed, then drain. Do this three times.

4. Put the container on its side where a reasonable room temperature— 17–21°C (60–70°F)—is maintained.

5. Every evening and morning, fill the jar with cold or tepid water, then drain it off.

6. Sprouts will be ready to eat in 3–4 days. Rinse well before using.

Sprouts may also be grown on absorbent moist material after being thoroughly washed. They must be moistened twice a day, but any surplus water drained off. Grown on absorbent material, the sprouts have to be cut, which is wasteful; with the jam jar method the whole sprout and seed can be eaten.

Sprouts grown in the dark will be white. Beans and sunflowers have a better flavour grown in the dark, while leafy sprouts such as alfalfa and cress are better grown in the light so that they are green. If sprouts have been grown in the dark, they can be 'greened' by leaving them in artificial light or indirect sunlight for a few hours.

Adzuki Beans are small red beans containing 25% protein, and are a rich source of the essential amino acids, lysine, plus iron, niacin and calcium. Sprout at a temperature of 22°C (72°F), and rinse 4 times a day. Harvest at 2·5 cm (1 in) length after about 4 days.

Alfalfa is widely cultivated for forage, and contains vitamins D, E, G, K and U. It is a rich source of amino acids and minerals and contains 35% protein. Alfalfa has a very high chlorophyll content which sweetens the breath. If harvested before green leaves appear, when the root is only 0·3 cm ($\frac{1}{8}$ in) long, it contains a concentrated percentage of protein. Sprout at a temperature of 22°C (72°F), rinsing twice a day. Harvest at 3·5–5 cm ($1\frac{1}{2}$–2 in) length, after 3–5 days.

Almond sprouts are crisp and crunchy, with 18% protein content in the nuts, which are rich in calcium and potassium. Sprout at 20–30°C (68–86°F), rinsing 2–3 times a day. Harvest when root is 0·5 cm ($\frac{1}{4}$ in) long after 3–4 days.

Barley sprouts are good in soups, salads and breads. Sprout at 21–27°C (70–80°F), rinsing 2–3 times a day. Harvest when root is length of seed after 3–4 days.

Beans of all kinds may be sprouted at 20–30°C (68–86°F), rinsing 3–4 times a day. Harvest at 2·5–5 cm (1–2 in) length after 3–5 days. They are a rich source of protein, and an excellent source of iron, phosphorus, potassium, vitamins B_1 and B_2, and calcium.

Chick Peas (Garbanzo) produce delicious sprouts. The peas have 20% protein, are a good source of iron and have trace quantities of vitamins A and C which are increased by sprouting. Sprout at 20–22°C (68–72°F), rinsing 4–6 times a day. Harvest when root is 1 cm ($\frac{1}{2}$ in) long after 3 days.

Corn (Maize) sprouts are deliciously sweet. Sprout at 22–30°C (72–86°F), rinsing 2–3 times a day. Harvest when root is 1 cm ($\frac{1}{2}$ in) long after 2–3 days.

Cress contains large amounts of vitamins A and C. Sprout at 10–20°C (50–68°F), rinsing twice a day. Harvest when sprouts are 3·5 cm ($1\frac{1}{2}$ in) long after 4 days.

Fenugreek has a spicy flavour, and the seeds and sprouts are rich in iron and vitamin A. The seeds are 29% protein. Sprout at 20–30°C (68–86°F), rinsing once or twice a day. Harvest at 7·5 cm (3 in) length after 4–5 days.

Flax seeds contain 23% protein and sizeable quantities of niacin, calcium and iron. Sprout at 20–26°C (68–78°F), rinsing 2–3 times daily. Harvest at 2·5–5 cm (1–2 in) after 4 days.

Lentils contain 25% protein, and substantial amounts of vitamin B, iron and phosphorous. Traces of vitamin C and E are increased when sprouted. Sprout at 20–30°C (68–86°F), rinsing 2–3 times daily. Harvest at 2·5 cm (1 in) after 3–4 days.

Millet has a sweet flavour and is the most alkaline of all cereals and therefore easily digested. It is rich in iron and niacin and a source of protein, phosphorus and vitamin B_2. Sprout at 21–27°C (70–80°F), rinsing 2–3 times daily. Harvest when root is 0·5 cm ($\frac{1}{4}$ in) after 3–4 days.

Mung (Chinese) Beans are a good source of choline and of vitamin E, both of which increase during sprouting. Sprout at 20–30°C (68–86°F), rinsing 3–4 times daily. Harvest at 5 cm (2 in) length after 3–4 days.

Oats contain 14% protein and all the essential amino acids. They are rich in vitamin C and have a good supply of minerals. They require little water for sprouting and tend to sour quickly. Sprout at 21–27°C (70–80°F), rinsing only enough to keep seeds moist. Harvest after 3–4 days, when the lead roots (the longest of the three) is the length of the oat seed.

Peas have 22% protein when dried and contain all the essential amino acids. Sprout at 10–20°C (50–68°F), rinsing 2–3 times daily. Harvest when root is length of seed after 3 days.

Pumpkin Seeds are very high in phosphorus and iron and contain 30% protein. Use hulled seeds for sprouting and do not oversprout. Sprout at 20–30°C (68–86°F), rinsing 2–3 times daily. Harvest when root is 0·5 cm ($\frac{1}{4}$ in) long after 3 days.

Rice may be sprouted and whole brown rice is best. It is an excellent source of niacin and contains an appreciable amount of vitamin E. Vitamin C is much increased during sprouting. Sprout at 10–27°C (50–80°F), rinsing 2–3 times daily. Harvest when root is length of seed after 3–4 days.

Rye is rich in manganese, phosphorus, potassium and iron, and contains 12% protein. Sprout at 10–20°C (50–68°F), rinsing 2–3 times daily. Harvest when root is length of seed after 3–4 days.

Sesame contains 18% protein and essential amino acids. The seeds also contain vitamin B_1, niacin and a small amount of vitamin E. Much calcium and lecithin in sesame makes it a valuable aid in preventing cholesterol from collecting in the blood. Sprout at 20–27°C (68–80°F), rinsing 4 times daily. Harvest when root is length of seed after 3 days.

Soybeans are an excellent meat substitute, containing up to 40% protein. They are rich in vitamin B and lecithin. They tend to ferment easily and can be difficult to sprout in hot weather, and they must be flooded several times daily with lukewarm water, then drained. Sprout only fresh seeds, at 20–30°C (68–86°F), rinsing every 3 hours. Harvest at 5 cm (2 in) length after 4 days.

Sunflower Seeds sprout quickly and easily, but should not be oversprouted as they develop a strong flavour. Sprout at 18–24°C (65–75°F), rinsing twice daily. Harvest when root is no longer than the seed after 24–36 hours.

Triticale is a cross between wheat and rye which contains more protein than any other cereal grain, as well as essential amino acids. Sprout at 20–30°C (68–86°F), rinsing twice daily. Harvest when roots are 0·5 cm ($\frac{1}{4}$ in) after 2–3 days.

Vegetable Seeds of many kinds can be sprouted and usually have the flavour of the vegetable. Cabbage, cauliflower, broccoli, mustard, turnip, lettuce and radish seeds are those most often sprouted. They are a good source of vitamins and minerals, and are low in calories. Sprout at 20–30°C (68–86°F), rinsing twice daily. Harvest at 2·5–5 cm (1–2 in) after 3–5 days.

Wheat is rich in vitamin E and its low vitamin C content is increased 600% when sprouted. Sprout at 21–27°C (70–80°F), rinsing twice daily. Harvest when roots are about 1 cm ($\frac{1}{2}$ in) long after 3–4 days.

Note : In the following recipes, quantities of sprouts are given in volume, not weight, measures.

Summer Tomato Soup

625 ml (1$\frac{1}{4}$ pints) tomato juice
2 tomatoes
1 slice green pepper
$\frac{1}{2}$ small cucumber
1 stick celery
1 spring onion
250 ml ($\frac{1}{2}$ pint) alfalfa sprouts

Put the tomato juice in a blender. Peel the tomatoes, remove the seeds, and cut up the flesh. Put the tomato flesh, pepper, cucumber, celery, onion and sprouts into the blender and blend until smooth. Serve chilled.

Tomato Soup

5 large tomatoes
50 g (2 oz) butter
1 bayleaf
pinch thyme
2 cloves
1 small onion
375 ml (¾ pint) water
15 g (½ oz) cornflour
pinch salt
125 ml (¼ pint) alfalfa sprouts
50 g (2 oz) grated Parmesan cheese

Skin the tomatoes and chop them. Put the butter into a saucepan and add the tomatoes, bayleaf, thyme, cloves and sliced onion. Simmer for 5 minutes. Remove the bayleaf and cloves and sieve the tomato mixture. Mix with the water and cornflour and simmer until thickened. Season with salt and stir in the alfalfa sprouts. Reheat and serve sprinkled with cheese.

Green Soup

6 green tomatoes
1 green pepper
1 small cucumber
4 tablespoons olive oil
1 garlic clove
pinch salt
2 tablespoons white vinegar
pinch cumin
375 ml (¾ pint) alfalfa sprouts
1 spring onion
50 ml (2 fl oz) iced water
125 ml (¼ pint) dry white wine

Skin the tomatoes and cut them in pieces. Mince the tomatoes, green pepper and unpeeled cucumber. Mix with olive oil, crushed garlic, salt, vinegar and cumin, and stir in the chopped alfalfa sprouts and finely chopped spring onion. Chill well. Just before serving, stir in the iced water and wine. Serve garnished with some chopped red tomato, or with small cubes of fried or toasted bread.

Fenugreek Soup

1 large potato
375 ml ($\frac{3}{4}$ pint) water
500 ml (1 pint) fenugreek sprouts
125 ml ($\frac{1}{4}$ pint) milk
salt

Boil the potato in the water until tender, drain, and reserve the liquid. Cut up the potato and put into a blender with the fenugreek sprouts, reserving a few, and milk, and blend until smooth. Put into a pan with the cooking water from the potato. Season and heat to boiling point. Garnish with the remaining sprouts.

Chicken and Bean Soup

50 g (2 oz) butter
1 small onion
2 sticks celery
2 medium-sized potatoes
625 ml (1$\frac{1}{4}$ pints) chicken stock
juice of $\frac{1}{2}$ lemon
salt and pepper
225 g (8 oz) cooked chicken
100 g (4 oz) sweetcorn kernels
125 ml ($\frac{1}{4}$ pint) Chinese bean sprouts
375 ml ($\frac{3}{4}$ pint) creamy milk
2 tablespoons chopped parsley

Heat the butter and cook the finely chopped onion and celery until soft but not brown. Cut the potatoes in cubes and add to the onions, stirring and cooking for 5 minutes. Add the chicken stock, lemon juice, salt and pepper. Bring to the boil, and simmer with a lid on until the vegetables are tender but not broken. Cut the chicken into small pieces and add to the soup with the corn kernels and bean sprouts. Continue simmering for 15 minutes. Add the milk and heat and serve hot sprinkled with parsley.

Green Rice Salad

225 g (8 oz) cooked long-grain rice
bunch watercress
2 tablespoons chopped chives
2 tablespoons chopped parsley
salt and pepper
125 ml ($\frac{1}{4}$ pint) fenugreek sprouts

4 tablespoons salad oil
2 tablespoons vinegar

Put the rice into a serving bowl. Add the chopped watercress leaves, chives, parsley, salt and pepper. Stir in the fenugreek sprouts. Just before serving, mix the oil and vinegar, pour over the salad, and toss well.

Mushroom Salad

175 g (6 oz) button mushrooms
250 ml (½ pint) Chinese bean sprouts
500 ml (1 pint) alfalfa sprouts
75 g (3 oz) peas
4 tablespoons salad oil
2 tablespoons lemon juice
1 garlic clove

Wipe the mushrooms and cut them in thin slices. Mix with the bean and alfalfa sprouts, and the uncooked peas. Mix together the salad oil, lemon juice and crushed garlic and pour over the salad.

Alfalfa Salad

4 sticks celery
250 ml (½ pint) alfalfa sprouts
100 g (4 oz) raisins
2 large carrots

For the dressing:
125 ml (¼ pint) yoghurt
3 tablespoons mayonnaise
1 teaspoon made mustard
pinch salt

Mix the finely chopped celery, alfalfa sprouts, raisins, grated carrots, and chill. Mix the yoghurt, mayonnaise, mustard and salt and chill until serving time. Arrange the salad on individual plates and pour over the yoghurt dressing.

Chinese Salad

250 ml (½ pint) Chinese bean sprouts
2 sticks celery
1 large carrot
50 g (2 oz) cashew nuts
1 tablespoon sesame seeds

2 tablespoons salad oil
1 tablespoon vinegar
watercress or lettuce

Mix the bean sprouts with finely chopped celery, grated carrots, chopped nuts and sesame seeds. Mix with the oil and vinegar and serve on a bed of watercress or lettuce.

Adzuki Salad

500 ml (1 pint) adzuki bean sprouts
2 tablespoons water
3 sticks celery
6 radishes
1 small unpeeled cucumber
1 small green pepper
6 crisp lettuce leaves
4 tablespoons salad oil
2 tablespoons vinegar

Put the sprouts into a saucepan with the water and simmer for 2 minutes. Cool and put into a bowl. Chop the celery, slice the radishes, dice the cucumber, chop the green pepper and shred the lettuce. Mix all the vegetables together and toss in the oil and vinegar just before serving.

Whole Earth Salad

250 ml ($\frac{1}{2}$ pint) alfalfa sprouts
250 ml ($\frac{1}{2}$ pint) Chinese bean sprouts
250 ml ($\frac{1}{2}$ pint) adzuki bean sprouts
100 g (4 oz) Cheddar cheese
1 cabbage lettuce
1 green pepper
3 spring onions
2 tablespoons chopped parsley
2 large tomatoes
1 avocado
4 tablespoons salad oil
2 tablespoons vinegar

Put the three kinds of sprouts into a salad bowl. Cut the cheese in cubes and add to the bowl. Tear the lettuce into pieces, chop the pepper, onions and parsley, and mix them all into the salad. Skin the tomatoes and remove the seeds. Chop the flesh and add to the salad together with the chopped avocado. Dress with oil and vinegar and serve at once.

Herbed Fish with Bean Sprouts

250 ml ($\frac{1}{2}$ pint) Chinese bean sprouts
2 tablespoons chopped parsley
1 tablespoon chopped chives
$\frac{1}{2}$ tablespoon chopped dill
450 g (1 lb) cod or haddock fillet
salt and pepper
50 g (2 oz) butter
juice of $\frac{1}{2}$ lemon

Grease the bottom of an ovenware dish. Mix the sprouts and herbs and sprinkle them on the bottom of the dish. Top with the fish in one piece. Sprinkle with salt and pepper, small flakes of butter and the lemon juice. Bake at 200°C (400°F)/Gas 6 for 25 minutes.

Alfalfa Omelette

6 eggs
50 ml (2 fl oz) milk
pinch salt
50 g (2 oz) grated Cheddar cheese
250 ml ($\frac{1}{2}$ pint) alfalfa sprouts
25 g (1 oz) butter

Separate the eggs. Mix the egg yolks, milk, salt, cheese and sprouts. Whisk the egg whites to stiff peaks and fold into the egg yolk mixture. Melt the butter in a heavy pan and pour in the egg mixture. Cook over low heat until firm, fold over and serve.

Stuffed Eggs

6 hard-boiled eggs
50 g (2 oz) butter
50 g (2 oz) grated Cheddar cheese
125 ml ($\frac{1}{4}$ pint) alfalfa sprouts

Cut the eggs in half lengthwise. Remove the yolks and cream with softened butter and the cheese. Add the alfalfa sprouts and stuff the mixture into the egg whites. Sprinkle with a few more sprouts.

Stuffed Tomatoes

6 large tomatoes
125 ml ($\frac{1}{4}$ pint) alfalfa sprouts

49

125 ml (¼ pint) Chinese bean sprouts
1 tablespoon chopped chives
2 tablespoons salad oil
1 tablespoon lemon juice
salt and pepper

Remove a small slice from the top of each tomato and scoop out the insides. Put the flesh through a sieve. Mix with chopped alfalfa and bean sprouts, chives, oil, juice and seasoning. Fill the tomatoes with the mixture and chill before serving.

Fenugreek Potatoes

450 g (1 lb) cooked potatoes
2 tablespoons oil
½ teaspoon turmeric powder
500 ml (1 pint) fenugreek sprouts
pinch cayenne pepper
pinch salt

Chop the potatoes. Heat the oil in a thick pan and add the potatoes and turmeric. Cook the potatoes for 5 minutes, stirring often. Add the fenugreek sprouts, cayenne pepper and salt, and continue to cook with a lid on for 5 minutes.

Beans and Sprouts

450 g (1 lb) young French beans
50 g (2 oz) butter
1 tablespoon oil
3 shallots
250 ml (½ pint) Chinese bean sprouts
2 tablespoons chopped parsley
salt and pepper
pinch ground nutmeg

Cook the beans whole until tender and drain well. Heat the butter and oil together in a heavy pan and add the chopped shallots. Cook gently for 3 minutes. Add the bean sprouts and stir quickly. Add the cooked beans and toss in the butter until the beans are hot. Sprinkle with parsley, salt and pepper and nutmeg and serve hot.

Curried Fenugreek

1 small onion
2 tablespoons oil

500 ml (1 pint) fenugreek sprouts
2 teaspoons curry powder
1 teaspoon cornflour
50 ml (2 fl oz) water

Chop the onion and fry it gently in the oil until transparent. Add the chopped fenugreek sprouts and curry powder and continue cooking for 2 minutes. Mix the cornflour and water and add to the sprouts. Simmer for 4 minutes until the mixture thickens.

Bean Sprout Sauce

100 g (4 oz) butter
1 garlic clove
225 g (8 oz) mushrooms
2 tablespoons chopped parsley
2 tablespoons chopped chives
125 ml (¼ pint) Chinese bean sprouts

Melt the butter and cook the crushed garlic for 2 minutes. Add the sliced mushrooms and cook over gentle heat, stirring well, for 5 minutes. Stir in the chopped parsley and chives, and the bean sprouts, and serve at once over boiled new potatoes.

Cottage Cheese Dip

100 g (4 oz) cottage cheese
pinch caraway seeds
1 garlic clove
125 ml (¼ pint) natural yoghurt
125 ml (¼ pint) fenugreek sprouts
salt

Sieve the cottage cheese. Mix with the caraway seeds, crushed garlic clove, yoghurt, finely chopped sprouts and salt. Chill for 2 hours in a serving bowl. Serve with crisps for dipping, or with fingers of carrots, celery and cucumber.

Cucumber Spread

1 small cucumber
1 small onion
225 g (8 oz) cream cheese
pinch salt
125 ml (¼ pint) fenugreek sprouts

Cut the unpeeled cucumber in half lengthwise and scoop out the seeds. Grate the cucumber and onion coarsely and drain away liquid in a sieve. Mix with cream cheese, salt and chopped fenugreek sprouts. Spread on biscuits or use for sandwiches.

Mushroom Spread

225 g (8 oz) mushrooms
50 g (2 oz) butter
1 tablespoon chopped chives
1 tablespoon chopped parsley
250 ml ($\frac{1}{2}$ pint) Chinese bean sprouts
pinch salt
15 g ($\frac{1}{2}$ oz) cornflour
2 tablespoons water

Cut the mushrooms into small pieces and cook in the butter until soft. Add the chopped herbs, chopped sprouts, salt, and cornflour mixed with water. Simmer for 3 minutes until the mixture is thick. Serve on rounds of wholemeal toast.

Cream Cheese Snacks

225 g (8 oz) cream cheese
2 tablespoons chopped chives
$\frac{1}{2}$ teaspoon made mustard
salt and pepper
125 ml ($\frac{1}{4}$ pint) fenugreek sprouts

Mix the cheese with the chives, mustard, salt and pepper. Chop the fenugreek sprouts and work into the cheese mixture. Shape into a long log and chill in the refrigerator. Slice into rounds and serve on slices of wholemeal bread.

Adzuki Pancakes

50 g (2 oz) coarse oatmeal
100 ml (4 fl oz) water
250 ml ($\frac{1}{2}$ pint) adzuki sprouts
2 eggs
1 small onion
pinch salt
oil for frying

Put the oatmeal in the water and leave for 2 hours. Mince the sprouts coarsely. Mix together the soaked oatmeal, minced sprouts, eggs, finely chopped onion and salt. Heat some oil in a thick frying pan and drop in spoonfuls of the mixture. Flatten the mixture slightly with the back of a spoon. Brown until golden on both sides.

Triticale Pancakes

100 g (4 oz) plain flour
pinch salt
1 teaspoon baking powder
1 teaspoon sugar
2 eggs
200 ml (8 fl oz) milk
125 ml ($\frac{1}{4}$ pint) Triticale sprouts
40 g (1$\frac{1}{2}$ oz) melted butter

Put flour, salt, baking powder and sugar into a bowl. Whisk the eggs and milk together and mix thoroughly into the dry ingredients. Add the finely chopped sprouts and melted butter. Cook small thick pancakes in butter or lard, browning on both sides.

Alfalfa Biscuits

175 g (6 oz) honey
100 g (4 oz) butter
few drops vanilla essence
100 g (4 oz) wholemeal flour
$\frac{1}{4}$ teaspoon bicarbonate of soda
$\frac{1}{2}$ teaspoon baking powder
225 g (8 oz) porridge oats
375 ml ($\frac{3}{4}$ pint) alfalfa sprouts

Cream the honey, butter and vanilla essence and work in the flour, soda and baking powder. Add oats and chopped sprouts and drop by spoonfuls on a greased baking sheet. Bake at 180°C (350°F)/Gas 4 for 12 minutes.

Alfalfa Cakes

225 g (8 oz) wholemeal flour
50 g (2 oz) sugar
1$\frac{1}{2}$ teaspoons baking powder
pinch salt
50 g (2 oz) honey
1 egg
200 ml (8 fl oz) milk

50 g (2 oz) melted butter
250 ml (½ pint) alfalfa sprouts

Mix the flour, sugar, baking powder and salt. Lightly whisk together the honey, egg, milk and butter, and add the chopped alfalfa sprouts. Mix into the flour. Put into small greased cake tins and bake at 200°C (400°F)/Gas 6 for 20 minutes.

Date and Nut Bread

175 g (6 oz) stoned dates
200 ml (8 fl oz) boiling water
225 g (8 oz) sugar
1 tablespoon melted butter
1 egg
175 g (6 oz) plain flour
1 teaspoon bicarbonate of soda
½ teaspoon baking powder
pinch salt
100 g (4 oz) chopped walnuts
125 ml (¼ pint) Triticale sprouts

Chop the dates and pour boiling water over them. Leave them to stand for 30 minutes. Mix together the sugar, butter and egg, and then stir in the flour, soda, baking powder and salt. Stir in the dates and water, and then the walnuts and finely chopped or minced Triticale sprouts. Mix thoroughly and put into two 450-g (1-lb) loaf tins. Bake at 180°C (350°F)/Gas 4 for 45 minutes. Cool on a rack, and serve in slices with butter.

The Salad Bowl

There is no excuse for the traditional salad bowl of limp lettuce leaves, wedges of soggy tomatoes, slices of hard-boiled egg and cucumber, dressed with acid vinegar and stained with beetroot. Mixed salads can be delicious, but their contents must be blended carefully and dressed with skill. The essence of a good salad is a blend of texture and appetising flavour. If soft ingredients such as beetroot or tomato are used, the palate appreciates something crisp or crunchy as a contrast. Raw vegetables, not usually thought of in the context of salads, are particularly useful for providing contrast—try finely shredded carrots or thinly sliced cabbage or chopped celery.

Cooked vegetables are also excellent in salads. Cooked dried beans, baby carrots, cooked peas and new potatoes can all be mixed with the more traditional ingredients. Sprouted seeds, either raw or lightly cooked (see Chapter 4), add another dimension to salads, and so do dried fruits plumped up in a little lemon juice, and whole or chopped nuts.

Another good kind of salad is made with single cooked vegetables tossed in French dressing. Best for this treatment are artichokes (either whole, or just the hearts), cauliflowers, courgettes, leeks and asparagus, lightly cooked and put into the dressing while still just warm.

Although many people still think of salad as an accompaniment to cold meat, fish, poultry, cheese or eggs, there is no reason why a salad cannot be served with a hot dish, particularly with grilled meat or fish, or with a rather creamy egg or cheese dish which needs a contrast in texture to be really appetising. When served with cold foods, salads can be complete meals if shellfish, grated or cubed cheese, cubed cold meat or chopped eggs are included with the vegetables. For those who like a completely vegetable meal, beans as a salad ingredient will supply essential protein.

It is worth remembering that an eminent nutritionist, Bircher-Benner, said that something fresh and raw at the beginning of a meal aids digestion and helps the body to utilise protein more efficiently, so that less is needed. It is well worth planning one salad in each day's menu, as a meal in itself, or at least as a small starter or an accompaniment to the main dish. Remember that many people prefer to make up their own salads from a variety of different vegetables, so that they can omit those ingredients they dislike.

Beetroot Traditionally beetroot is boiled until tender, but it tastes much better if it is baked instead. Whichever way you prefer to cook it, choose small beetroot of even size, wash them well and leave about 2·5-cm (1-in) stems. Put into an ovenware dish and bake without liquid at 180°C (350°F)/Gas 4 for 30 minutes, and then at 160°C (325°F)/Gas 3 for 1 hour. Alternatively, boil in water for the same length of time without breaking the skins. Peel while still hot and dress with vinegar if liked. Avoid mixing beetroot with other vegetables because the colour runs so badly.

Celery and Celeriac Clean celery well and remove any strings. Leave to stand in iced water to become very crisp before chopping finely and adding to salads. Celeriac has a root like turnip but tastes like celery heart. Scrub thoroughly, peel thinly, and then grate coarsely. Dress at once with lemon juice because celeriac discolours quickly, then toss in a little French dressing before using.

Chicory Chicory may be used as individual leaves, or cut across into rings for salad, but when cut the vegetable discolours very quickly. It should never be left to soak in water or it becomes very bitter. Serve in a French dressing or add to a green salad. Chicory blends particularly well with fresh orange slices and with olives.

Cucumber Cucumbers should never be peeled before slicing as they are more digestible with the skin on, and the skin contains the main food value. Slice cucumber very thinly, sprinkle with a little salt and leave for an hour before draining and adding to salads. A good dressing for cucumber is a mixture of equal parts of white vinegar and water, seasoned with salt, pepper and a pinch of sugar, and garnished with chopped parsley or dill.

Endive The foliage of endive is rather bitter and crisp and it makes a refreshing salad with French dressing, or mixed with other greenstuff. Rinse the leaves and chill them before serving. Endive tends to grow rather large, so use just a few leaves from a plant at a time. In this way, the whole plant need not be destroyed.

Lettuce Lettuce leaves should be eaten while young and crisp and not allowed to become old and leathery. They should not be cut, but should be torn in pieces after thorough washing and drying. Lettuce makes an excellent salad on its own, with French dressing containing a hint of mustard and sugar, but it also mixes well with other greenstuff and a sprinkling of herbs.

Potatoes The best potatoes for salad should be 'waxy' and just cooked but not broken. Dressing should be added while the potatoes are still hot, so that they absorb the flavour. A good potato salad can be made with the potatoes tossed in fresh hot bacon fat, plus a little crisp crumbled bacon and finely chopped onion or chives. Tiny new potatoes are excellent tossed in French dressing with some chopped onions and green peppers added.

Radishes Radishes are excellent on their own, eaten whole with a smear of unsalted butter. When they have been cleaned, radishes should be left in a bowl of ice-cold water before adding whole or thinly sliced to salads.

Spring Onions These popular little onions may be left whole in salads, with the green tips trimmed, or they can be sliced in thin rings and mixed with other salad vegetables, or served on their own in French dressing. They are good added to potato salad, or mixed with orange segments or slices in French dressing.

Tomatoes For perfect salads, tomatoes need to be skinned. Do this by holding each tomato with a fork over a flame, or else by dipping them in hot and then cold water. The skins should then be easy to remove. Slice tomatoes into French dressing with a garnish of chopped basil or mint and a little chopped onion. A good mixture can be made of alternate layers of sliced tomatoes and sliced hard-boiled eggs in a bowl, served with mayonnaise or French dressing. Very large tomatoes can be hollowed out and filled with raw or cooked vegetables to serve as individual salads.

French Dressing

2 tablespoons wine vinegar or lemon juice
salt and pepper

pinch dry mustard
6 tablespoons olive or salad oil

Put the vinegar into a bowl with the salt, pepper and mustard, stir well and slowly add the oil, beating until well mixed. The oil will come to the top when the dressing is left to stand but can be beaten again just before serving. A large quantity of this dressing can be made and stored in the refrigerator in a screwtop jar; the jar should be shaken well before each use. Some people like to add a pinch of sugar, and some freshly chopped herbs to this dressing.

Salad Cream

100 g (4 oz) margarine
75 g (3 oz) plain flour
75 g (3 oz) sugar
15 g ($\frac{1}{2}$ oz) mustard powder
750 ml (1$\frac{1}{2}$ pints) milk
2 eggs
375 ml ($\frac{3}{4}$ pint) vinegar
salt and pepper

Melt the margarine over a low heat. Remove from the heat and work in the flour, sugar, mustard and a little milk. Return to the heat and gradually add the remaining milk, stirring all the time until the mixture is thick and smooth. Take off the heat and beat well. Cool and beat in the eggs, and then slowly beat in the vinegar a little at a time. Season with salt and pepper. Put into screwtop jars and store in a cool place. This will keep up to six weeks and is popular with people who find mayonnaise too rich.

Easy Mayonnaise

1 egg
1 tablespoon vinegar or lemon juice
$\frac{1}{2}$ teaspoon salt
$\frac{1}{4}$ teaspoon pepper
$\frac{1}{4}$ teaspoon mustard powder
1 teaspoon sugar
$\frac{1}{2}$ pint olive or salad oil

Put the egg, vinegar or lemon juice and seasonings into a bowl and stir into a paste. Slowly beat in the oil drop by drop until the mixture is thick. This is a creamy mayonnaise which can also be made very quickly in an electric blender.

58

Cole Slaw

Shred raw white-hearted cabbage finely and mix with grated carrot, chopped apple, chopped celery, grated onion, a few raisins and nuts. Dress with home-made salad cream seasoned with a little extra mustard.

Swedish Salad

Shred some red cabbage and mix with a little grated apple and onion. Dress with French dressing and garnish with chopped dill or parsley.

Carrot Salads

Mix coarsely grated carrot with French dressing and a mixture of chopped fresh herbs. Try mixing grated onion and carrots in oil with salt and pepper. Fresh lemon juice or orange juice with a pinch of sugar and a little chopped parsley make a good dressing for carrots.

Cucumber Salads

Stir thinly sliced cucumber into natural yoghurt flavoured with crushed garlic and garnished with chopped mint. A mixture of cucumber and thinly sliced radishes is good dressed with French dressing made with lemon juice and seasoned with a little crushed garlic, mint, salt and pepper and a pinch of sugar.

Spinach Salads

Use well-washed young tender spinach leaves, shake dry and chill. Dress with French dressing containing plenty of crushed garlic and mustard, and a little chopped onion. Try mixing spinach leaves with thinly sliced raw mushrooms in French dressing, topped with crumbled crisp bacon.

Celery Salads

Chill celery sticks in iced water, chop in small pieces and mix with chopped hard-boiled egg in French dressing with plenty of herbs. Try grated celeriac mixed with diced apple, or chopped celery and walnuts in a mixture of mayonnaise and whipped cream.

Culinary Herbs

Once upon a time, some 400 herbs were in regular use for culinary and medicinal purposes. The Victorians were still using about 40 herbs regularly, but today few gardens can boast more than half a dozen, and many people make do with only mint and parsley. This seems a pity, when herb plants are highly decorative as well as full of flavour, and many of them are attractive in both flower and vegetable gardens. There is no need for a special herb garden if space is limited, and indeed a good selection of culinary herbs can be grown in a single large tub, a window-box, or a series of pots on a path, in a greenhouse, or even on a kitchen window-sill.

Herbs are easy to grow and not too fussy about soil and conditions. Mint and angelica like moist soil, while parsley needs a rich soil and fennel prefers open ground. Many other types actually like poor dry land, but they all love sunshine to bring out their aromatic qualities. Most herbs can be grown from seeds, but some are best grown from the division of older plants. Where a plant can be grown by both methods, the root division gives quicker results. For ease of cultivation, grow herbs near a path where they may be easily tended and harvested. Hoe between the plants regularly to keep the ground clean and light, and trim perennial plants such as thyme and sage in the autumn to keep neat shapes—the trimmed leaves can of course be dried for winter use. Culinary and medicinal herbs are grown in the same way, but uses for medicinal herbs are detailed in Chapter 12.

Angelica (*perennial*) has a reputation as an antiseptic, and was claimed to be a protection against evil. Seeds germinate slowly and should be kept in moist sand before sowing in August, or should be used straight from the plant. Candy the stems, or use them as a flavouring for rhubarb dishes.

Balm (*perennial*) is also known as lemon balm and Melissa, and has a lemon scent. It was reputed to strengthen the brain and drive out melancholy as well as improve the memory. Plants increase rapidly and can be invasive. Use in stuffings and salads, and in scented herb mixtures for *pot pourri*.

Basil (*annual*) has a sweet clove flavour, but the reputation of being a cursed plant. It was believed that basil would only flourish if tended by a beautiful woman. Plant the seeds in gentle heat in March, prick off into boxes, and plant in rich warm soil or in pots, in June. Basil is a tender plant which dislikes cold. Use it with tomatoes, liver and sausages.

Bay leaves were used to crown the heroes of ancient Greece and Rome, and the trees can grow to enormous proportions, reputedly keeping away the devil, thunder and lightning. Small bay trees may be purchased, but it is difficult to increase stock, and this is best done by layering the lower branches of a tree. The leaves form part of a *bouquet garni*, and are excellent in beef and fish dishes and milk puddings, but should be used sparingly.

Borage (*annual*) is sometimes known as the herb of courage, or the herb of gladness, because it was reputed to raise the spirits. It grows easily from seed and spreads rapidly, so can be invasive. The bright blue flowers and cucumber-flavoured leaves are mainly used for flavouring and decorating long summer drinks.

Caraway seed (*biennial*) were once a favourite flavouring, reputed to be an aid to digestion and to sweeten the breath. Sow the seeds in autumn or spring, and harvest them in July. Use in cakes, sweets and biscuits, and in cabbage dishes.

Chervil (*biennial*) looks like parsley but has a more delicate flavour. Sow small successions of seeds from early spring to autumn, watering well in dry weather. Use for salads, egg and fish dishes. Chervil does not dry or freeze well as the flavour is so delicate.

Chives (*perennial*) have a light onion flavour and are very useful for flavouring and garnishing. Divide clumps of small bulbs in spring or autumn, and lift and replant every 2 years. Do not let the plant run to flower but trim off buds as they appear. Use for salads, egg dishes, cream cheese, soups and vinegars.

Coriander (*annual*) has a scent of orange and curry, and is a main ingredient in curry powder. Sow seeds in April, and cut down the plant when the seeds begin to ripen, leaving in a warm place to dry before removing the seeds. Use the seeds in sweets and curries, and the leaves in soups and stews.

Dill (*annual*) is a highly aromatic herb with digestive and sedative qualities. Both the seeds and leaves can be used in cookery. Sow the seeds in March and thin out the plants well. The flavour is particularly popular in Scandinavia and Central Europe, and is excellent with new potatoes, fish (especially salmon), and cucumber dishes.

Fennel (*perennial*) was regarded as one of the nine sacred herbs by the Anglo-Saxons, and was reputed to guard against unseen evil. It was used to restore sight, and also to aid slimming. Sow the seeds in April or May, but expect uneven germination. Use the leaves for fish, salads, pickles and vinegar.

Horseradish grows into a large plant with long roots which have to be grated for use. Plant single crowns with young roots 15 cm (6 in) long in well-prepared soil trenched with a dressing of well-rotted manure. Spring plants will give good roots in autumn, which can be lifted and stored in sand. Clean a root and grate to use in sauce or in flavoured vinegar (the root is as bad as onions for making the eyes sting and water).

Lovage (*perennial*) has a celery flavour which is hot and spicy, and grows into a large plant which likes plenty of water. Sow the plants in spring, or grow them from fresh seed, like angelica. Use the leaves in soups, casseroles and stews.

Marjoram (*perennial*) has preserving and disinfectant qualities, and was used for digestive disorders and toothache. It was one of the traditional herbs for 'strewing' on the floors of houses and is highly aromatic. The plant is tender and although it is a perennial, seeds may have to be sown annually. Use in force-meats, soups and stews. *Oregano* is a member of the marjoram family, but has a hotter and more pungent flavour and is generally grown in warm countries.

Mint (*perennial*) comes in dozens of varieties, but round-leaved (Lamb Mint) is best for traditional mint sauce. Eau-de-Cologne, Apple Mint,

Pineapple and Spearmint are highly aromatic and may be used for *pot pourri*, or for fruit salads. A bunch of mint in the kitchen helps to keep away flies (it was reputed to repel fleas in the Middle Ages, and was used as a 'strewing' herb). Plant in early spring by division of the roots, but confine in a bed away from other plants as mint spreads rapidly. Use in mint sauce, on vegetables, in salads, fruit salads, and for making savoury jelly.

Oregano See Marjoram

Parsley (*biennial*) is a most useful flavouring herb connected with many legends. Seeds sown on Good Friday will bring happiness and good fortune, but plants should not be transplanted or they will bring ill-luck. It is reputed that where parsley flourishes, the woman of the house is in command. Plant parsley seeds around an onion bed to keep away onion fly. Parsley takes a long time to germinate, and it is recommended that the seed should be sown along with a batch of radishes which grow and mature quickly and will mark the row. By the time the radishes are ready to harvest, the parsley will be growing well. It likes well-drained soil in a semi-shady position. Use for garnishing and for flavouring fish, ham, chicken, and for stuffings and sauces.

Rosemary (*perennial*) for remembrance, known for its legendary association with the Virgin Mary. The shrub is highly aromatic, and may be burned as incense, and always used to be planted near rue, the medicinal herb. Grow from cuttings in well-drained sheltered soil. Use for beef stews, for roasting duck, lamb or pork, and for mushrooms dishes.

Sage (*perennial*) aids digestion and was reputed to ensure long life. Grow from seed or root division, and look out for some of the many different kinds such as silver-leaved, golden and red sage which make beautiful plants. Use with rich meats such as pork, goose, duck and sausages.

Savory comes in two varieties, Winter Savory which is a perennial, and Summer Savory which is an annual raised from seed and which has a more subtle flavour. Savory is particularly used with broad beans.

Tarragon (*perennial*) can be grown from cuttings or root division. The French variety should be grown rather than the Russian, which is coarser in flavour. An essential ingredient in fine cooking, particularly for chicken, fish and sauces.

Thyme (*perennial*) was known as the enchanted herb, and was used as a remedy for melancholy. Like sage, it comes in many varieties which are decorative as well as useful. Grow from seed or from root division, and look out for Lemon Thyme which has a particularly delicious flavour. Use in forcemeats and stuffings.

COOKING WITH HERBS

Dried herbs are stronger in flavour than fresh ones: $\frac{1}{2}$ teaspoon dried herbs equals 2 teaspoons fresh herbs. If fresh herbs are chopped or crushed before cooking, they release their aromatic oils. Dried herbs should be crushed, or soaked for a few minutes in the liquid in the recipe.

A **bouquet garni** consists of thyme, parsley and a bayleaf, but sometimes marjoram is added. It is worth making up a number of 'bouquets' tied with cotton which can be stored in the freezer. If dried herbs are used, make up tiny muslin bags of the mixture and store them in jars ready for use.

Fines herbes, which are often specified for salads and for egg dishes, consist of chopped parsley, chervil, chives and tarragon chopped finely.

Mixed herbs usually consist of chopped sage, parsley and marjoram mixed with the small leaves of thyme.

Many foods have a special affinity with individual herbs, and the choice can rest on the family's taste. Herb flavouring should never be so powerful that it overshadows the food it accompanies, but the correct herb helps to bring out flavour, and often aids digestion, such as sage with pork or goose. The following list shows which herbs best complement basic foodstuffs.

Beef : marjoram, rosemary, savory, thyme

Cheese Dishes (hot) : basil, marjoram, tarragon, thyme

Cream Cheese : basil, caraway, chives, dill, mint, sage

Eggs : basil, chervil, chives, marjoram, tarragon, thyme

Fish : basil, chervil, chives, dill, fennel, mint, parsley, sage, thyme

Fruit : borage, lemon balm, mint, rosemary

Lamb : dill, marjoram, mint, rosemary, savory

Pickles : dill, tarragon

Poultry : marjoram, parsley, sage, savory, tarragon, thyme

Salads : basil, borage, chervil, chives, dill, fennel, lemon balm, mint, parsley, savory, tarragon

Veal : rosemary, sage, savory, thyme

Vegetables : basil, chives, fennel, mint, parsley, rosemary, savory, tarragon

64

DRYING HERBS

The best herbs for drying are sage, thyme, marjoram, tarragon, mint and bay. Gather the herbs just before they come into flower, and early in the day when the dew has just dried. Tie them loosely in small bunches and cover lightly with muslin or thin paper. Hang in a dry place where the air can circulate. When completely dry, leave bayleaves whole, but crush the other herbs with a rolling pin and pack in airtight tins or jars.

Parsley needs different treatment as it must be dried quickly to keep green. Wash parsley in cold water, shake well, and take leaves from the main stems. Spread on a wire rack and dry at 190°C (375°F)/Gas 5 for 4 minutes. Cool and crush the leaves and store.

FREEZING HERBS

Wash fresh herbs and pack in small bunches in foil or polythene. As an alternative, chop the herbs and pack into ice-cube trays with a little water. Freeze until solid, then release cubes, wrap them in foil, and store in polythene bags. The whole herbs can be used straight from the freezer, but are not suitable for garnishing, as they wilt quickly. The herb cubes may be added while still frozen to stews or sauces, or they can be put into a colander to thaw and drain before the chopped herbs are used.

Herb Seasoning

50 g (2 oz) dried orange peel
25 g (1 oz) marjoram
25 g (1 oz) thyme
25 g (1 oz) hyssop

To dry the orange peel, remove it in thin strips from the fruit without taking off the white pith. Dry at the bottom of a cool oven until crisp and then reduce the peel to powder with a rolling pin or an electric blender.

Dry the herbs and rub them down to a coarse powder. Mix well together and store in a tightly-covered jar. Use a couple of pinches of herb seasoning in stuffings and in meat dishes.

Sweet Herb Seasoning

50 g (2 oz) dried parsley
50 g (2 oz) dried marjoram
50 g (2 oz) dried chervil
25 g (1 oz) dried thyme
25 g (1 oz) dried lemon thyme
25 g (1 oz) dried basil

25 g (1 oz) dried savory
15 g (½ oz) dried tarragon

Mix together all the herbs and rub them to a coarse powder. Mix well and store in a tightly-covered jar. Use a couple of pinches of herb seasoning when mixed herbs are required for a recipe.

Herb Vinegars

Flavoured vinegars are excellent for salad dressings and for making mayonnaise. Use either cider vinegar or white wine vinegar and freshly picked herbs. Pick the leaves before the plants flower, and pack them into a wide-mouthed jar, bruising them slightly with a wooden spoon. Bring vinegar to boiling point and pour over the leaves. Cover tightly and leave to stand in a warm place for 10 days, shaking the jar occasionally. Drain off the vinegar and fill bottles, filtering the vinegar through muslin or filter paper. For a very strong flavour, pour the vinegar over a second batch of herbs, without boiling first, and leave for 10 days more before straining and bottling. Usually 250 ml (½ pint) herb leaves will flavour 500 ml (1 pint) vinegar. Tarragon, fennel, mint, marjoram, basil and dill are all good flavourings for vinegar.

Herb Jelly

2·7 kg (6 lb) apples
450 g (1 lb) fresh mint leaves
sugar
green vegetable colouring

Cut the apples in quarters, including the skins and cores. Chop the mint leaves thoroughly and put apples and mint into a large saucepan. Cover with cold water and bring to the boil. Simmer until the apples are completely soft. Put the mixture into a jelly bag or a clean tea towel and leave to drain overnight. Measure the liquid and allow 450 g (1 lb) sugar to each 500 ml (1 pint). Put liquid and sugar into a large pan and stir over gentle heat until the sugar has dissolved. Bring to the boil, and boil rapidly to setting point when tested on a cold saucer. Add a few drops of green vegetable colouring, stirring in well. Pour into small hot jars and cover when cold. Serve with lamb. If liked, a few of the chopped mint leaves may be reserved and added to the jelly just before potting.

The same recipe may be used to make parsley, sage, thyme or bayleaf jelly. These are all delicious as accompaniments to the appropriate meats or poultry, for example parsley with ham, and sage with pork.

Parsley Honey

100 g (4 oz) fresh parsley
625 ml (1¼ pints) water
450 g (1 lb) sugar
1 dessertspoon white vinegar

Wash the parsley very thoroughly and chop it up roughly, including the stalks. Put into a thick pan with the water and bring to the boil. Simmer gently until the liquid has been reduced to 500 ml (1 pint). Strain the liquid and put it into a clean saucepan with the sugar. Stir well and when the sugar has dissolved, bring it to the boil. Add the vinegar and simmer for about 30 minutes until the mixture is like clear honey. Pour into small jars and cover. This is very good as a spread on wholemeal bread, or it can be used to sweeten fruit salads.

Candied Angelica

fresh angelica stems
7 g (¼ oz) salt
2 litres (4 pints) water
sugar

The angelica stems should be used in April when they are tender. Cut the stems from the plant and cut into 7·5-cm (3-in) pieces. Dissolve the salt in the water and bring to the boil. Pour this hot brine over the angelica stems and leave for 10 minutes. Drain well and rinse in cold water. Put the stems into fresh boiling water and boil for 7 minutes until tender. Drain and scrape off the outer skin. Weigh the stems and take an equal weight of sugar. Allow 500 ml (1 pint) water for each 450 g (1 lb) sugar. Dissolve the sugar in water, bring to the boil and pour over the stems. Leave for 24 hours.

Bring to the boil again and take out the stems. Take 450 g (i lb) sugar for each original 450 g (1 lb) angelica and add it to the syrup. Bring to the boil and pour over the stems. Leave for 24 hours, then repeat the process.

Do this three more times, and then leave the stems to soak in the syrup for 14 days. Drain very well, and put on a wire rack lined with greaseproof paper. Dry very slowly in a warm place such as an airing cupboard or over a cooker.

Crystallised Mint Leaves

fresh mint leaves
1 egg white
granulated sugar

Choose large, well-shaped, fresh green mint leaves and wipe them dry very gently with kitchen paper. Beat the egg white to stiff peaks and coat both sides of each leaf. Dip the leaves into sugar until well covered, and put them on a wire rack covered with wax paper (use the lining paper from a cereal packet). Leave in a warm dry place until crisp. Store in an airtight container between layers of wax paper. Use to garnish fruit dishes and ice cream.

Winter Mint Sauce

> *100 g (4 oz) mint leaves*
> *100 g (4 oz) sugar*
> *250 ml ($\frac{1}{2}$ pint) vinegar*

Strip the mint leaves from the stems and put them into a colander. Pour boiling water over and then dry the leaves in a cloth. Sprinkle with 25 g (1 oz) sugar and chop finely. Put the vinegar and remaining sugar into a saucepan and simmer for 3 minutes until the sugar has dissolved. Pack the mint leaves into small jars and pour over the vinegar to cover the leaves by 1 cm ($\frac{1}{2}$ in). Seal with vinegar-proof lids. To use, dilute with a little more vinegar.

Herb Butter

> *1 teaspoon chopped parsley*
> *$\frac{1}{2}$ teaspoon chopped mint*
> *$\frac{1}{2}$ teaspoon chopped chives*
> *$\frac{1}{2}$ teaspoon chopped tarragon*
> *$\frac{1}{2}$ teaspoon chopped marjoram*
> *3 teaspoons lemon juice*
> *100 g (4 oz) butter*

Make sure all the herbs are chopped finely and put them into the lemon juice, stirring until they are well mixed. Cream the butter until soft and light and work in the herbs and lemon juice. Leave at room temperature for 2 hours so that the flavours penetrate the butter. Store in a covered jar in the refrigerator, and use for toast, rolls or sandwiches, or on steak, chops or fish.

Herb Bread

Use a crusty French loaf for preference and slash through it in 5-cm (2-in) slices, not quite cutting to the bottom of the loaf. Spread herb butter between the slices. Press the bread back into shape, wrap in foil and bake at 190°C (375°F)/Gas 5 for 25 minutes. Serve hot with salads, soup, meat or fish.

Herb Cheese

225 g (8 oz) grated Cheddar cheese
15 g (½ oz) chopped parsley
15 g (½ oz) chopped chives
15 g (½ oz) chopped thyme
15 g (½ oz) chopped sage
15 g (½ oz) chopped summer savory
2 tablespoons double cream
4 tablespoons dry sherry

Mix all the ingredients thoroughly and press into small pots. Cover and chill in the refrigerator. Use for sandwiches, toast or party snacks. This will keep up to 5 days in the refrigerator.

Herb Cream Cheese

100 g (4 oz) cream cheese
1 garlic clove
15 g (½ oz) chopped parsley
15 g (½ oz) chopped thyme
15 g (½ oz) chopped chives
salt and pepper

Cream the cheese with a fork and work in the crushed garlic clove and chopped herbs. Season well with salt and pepper and shape the cheese into a flattened ball. Chill. This is very good with wholemeal bread.

Seven Herb Cheese

2 tablespoons mixed fresh herbs
100 g (4 oz) grated Cheddar cheese
2 tablespoons double cream
3 tablespoons sherry
salt and pepper

The herbs to use are parsley, sage, thyme, tarragon, chives, chervil and summer savory, all finely chopped. Put all the ingredients into a double saucepan and stir over a gentle heat until the mixture is creamy and pale green. Fill small pots with the cheese and leave until cold before using. Serve with salad, or on crusty bread.

Herb Stuffings

50 g (2 oz) butter
1 small onion

75 g (3 oz) soft white breadcrumbs
1 lemon
salt and pepper
3 tablespoons fresh herbs
1 egg

There are many combinations of herbs which are excellent for stuffing meat, poultry and fish. A mixture of thyme, parsley and marjoram is a useful one for most purposes. A good stuffing should be light and crumbly when mixed, so avoid putting in too much liquid. When a joint of meat, a whole fish, or a bird are cooked, they lose a lot of cooking juices, which seep into the stuffing and give it flavour. If the stuffing is like a solid pudding when mixed, it will become heavy and indigestible when cooked, so that a very light hand is needed in the mixing.

Melt the butter and soften the finely chopped onion until it is golden. Mix with the breadcrumbs, grated lemon rind and juice, seasoning and chopped fresh herbs. Mix with the egg very lightly. If liked, a little chopped bacon, or poultry liver may be added.

Herb Sauce

25 g (1 oz) butter
25 g (1 oz) plain flour
500 ml (1 pint) milk
salt and pepper
2 tablespoons herbs

The liquid used can be all milk, or a mixture of milk and water. If ham, chicken or fish have been cooked in liquid, this stock may be used, but should be avoided if there is too much salt in it, which may happen if ham has been cooked. Parsley is the herb to use for ham, chicken or fish; fennel or dill may be used for fish, or for vegetables.

Melt the butter and work in the flour, cooking for 3 minutes. Gradually add the liquid and stir over low heat until the sauce is smooth. Season to taste and add the finely chopped herbs. A little extra butter or a spoonful of cream added just before serving will give extra flavour and a smooth sheen to the sauce.

Herb Dumplings

100 g (4 oz) self-raising flour
50 g (2 oz) shredded suet
salt and pepper
1 small onion
1 teaspoon fresh herbs

Mix together the flour, suet and seasoning and add just enough cold water to make a sticky dough. Add the grated onion and chopped herbs. Divide into 16 pieces and roll into small balls with floured hands. Simmer for 20 minutes in soups, stews, or the broth of boiled ham, chicken or salt beef.

Herb Flan

2 tablespoons fresh herbs
25 g (1 oz) grated Cheddar cheese
225 g (8 oz) shortcrust pastry
100 g (4 oz) lean bacon
2 eggs
250 ml ($\frac{1}{2}$ pint) milk
1 small onion
salt and pepper

Make as wide a selection of fresh herbs as possible. A mixture of chives, parsley, tarragon, lovage, chervil and marjoram is good, and they should be chopped finely together. Mix the cheese into the pastry and roll out to line a flan ring or pie plate. Chop the bacon finely and sprinkle on the base of the pastry. Beat together the eggs and milk lightly and add the finely chopped onion, chopped herbs and seasoning. Pour into the pastry case and bake at 200°C (400°F)/Gas 6 for 35 minutes. A little extra grated cheese may be sprinkled on top of the flan before baking if liked.

Fish Pie with Herbs

900 g (2 lb) cod or haddock
1 small onion
parsley, chives and basil
50 g (2 oz) butter
15 g ($\frac{1}{2}$ oz) plain flour
salt and pepper
2 hard-boiled eggs
175 g (6 oz) puff pastry
egg yolk for glazing

Simmer the fish with the chopped onion in 250 ml ($\frac{1}{2}$ pint) water, until the fish is just tender but not broken. Drain, reserving the liquid. Remove skin and bones, and break the fish into flakes. Put into a greased pie-dish with the onion. Sprinkle with 1 tablespoon herbs. Melt the butter, work in the flour and cook for 2 minutes. Add the reserved stock and stir until smooth. Season to taste and stir in the chopped hard-boiled eggs. Pour over the fish and mix lightly with a fork. Cover with pastry and brush with beaten egg yolk. Bake at 220°C (425°F)/Gas 7 for 30 minutes.

Soft Fruit

Soft fruit can be grown in the smallest garden, and is a worthwhile investment as it is increasingly difficult to buy in the shops, and is often of poor quality. Two or three gooseberry and blackcurrant bushes, one or two redcurrants grown in bush form or trained on a wall, a blackberry and a loganberry cane, a short row of raspberries and strawberries grown with the flowers or as a path edging will provide enough fruit to eat fresh, with some surplus for freezing and jam-making.

Even small daily quantities of each fruit can be used, turned into shortcakes or easily-made ices. Summer fruits have a happy knack of going together rather well, so that a few ounces of each fruit can be mixed to provide a large summer fruit bowl. For more elaborate dishes, a few raspberries may be enlivened with a sauce made of sweetened strawberry purée. Likewise strawberries are delicious with raspberry sauce, while redcurrants blend equally well with each fruit. Fresh fruit with caster sugar and cream is perhaps our favourite summer dish, but thin honey or a well-chilled egg custard can be used instead.

Soft Fruit Fools and Flummeries

Fruit fools are an essential part of summer eating. The simplest fool is made with a mixture of fruit and cream, and these days we usually sieve the fruit. Traditionally, however, the fruit was only lightly crushed before it was mixed with the cream. The fruit may be folded into softly whipped cream, or single cream; sometimes egg custard is used, although this blurs the taste of the fruit. Gooseberries, currants and blackberries are best simmered with a little water and sugar before sieving, but strawberries and raspberries should not be cooked before being sieved to a purée. Fools are at their best served chilled, with small sweet biscuits or sponge fingers. An old-fashioned dish which is similar to a fool is a flummery. This is thickened with a cereal such as barley or semolina, and is firm enough to be unmoulded before serving.

Soft Fruit Syrups

Syrups made from summer fruit and sugar can be bottled or frozen, and are invaluable as a basis of drinks and sauces, or as a flavouring for mousses, ices and other puddings. The best bottles to use are those with lever stoppers with a china cap and rubber washer, or sauce-bottles with screwtops. Syrups must be sterilised and stored in a cool dark place so that the colours do not fade. It is much easier and safer to store syrups in the freezer. They should be cooled and poured into 125-ml ($\frac{1}{4}$-pint) or 250-ml ($\frac{1}{2}$-pint) containers, leaving headspace, or they can be frozen in ice-cube trays. Individual cubes should be wrapped in foil, and a number of cubes put into polythene bags for storage. One syrup cube will provide a single portion for a drink or for sauce.

Make syrups from individual fruits, or from a mixture. Blackberries, blackcurrants, raspberries and strawberries are the most popular flavours. Use clean ripe fruit, and do not wash it is possible. Add 125 ml ($\frac{1}{4}$ pint) water to 1·35 kg (3 lb) raspberries, strawberries or blackberries, but 250 ml ($\frac{1}{2}$ pint) water to 1·35 kg (3 lb) blackcurrants. Simmer gently for 1 hour, crushing the fruit with a wooden spoon from time to time. Drain through a jellybag or clean tea towel overnight and measure the juice. Stir in 350 g (12 oz) sugar to each 500 ml (1 pint) juice until completely dissolved. Freeze at this point. If syrup has to be bottled, put into the bottles and put on tops. Stand bottles in a steriliser or preserving pan and fill with cold water to cover. Heat slowly so that the water reaches 80°C (175°F) within 1 hour. Continue at this heat for 30 minutes, remove the bottles, cool and store.

Summer Fruit Bowl

225 g (8 oz) strawberries
100 g (4 oz) blackcurrants
100 g (4 oz) redcurrants
225 g (8 oz) raspberries
175 g (6 oz) caster sugar

Hull the strawberries and remove the currants from their stems. Mix all the fruit in a serving bowl, sprinkling on sugar. Leave to stand in a cold place for at least 2 hours before serving. If a few sweet black cherries are available, stone them and add to the mixture.

For a special occasion, sprinkle with a little blackcurrant liqueur (cassis), or kirsch.

Baked Summer Fruit

450 g (1 lb) soft fruit
100 g (4 oz) sugar or honey
50 g (2 oz) butter

It always seems a pity to cook summer fruit, and there is nothing nastier than stewing it in water. On a cold evening however, a hot fruit dish may be welcome, or such a dish can make a pleasant change for a party. Use an earthenware casserole for the best flavour.

Clean and prepare the fruit and arrange in layers in the casserole with the sugar or honey, and flakes of butter. Cover with a lid or foil and cook at 170°C (325°F)/Gas 3 for 45 minutes until the fruit is soft but unbroken. Serve hot or cold with cream.

Soft Fruit Shortcake

100 g (4 oz) butter
100 g (4 oz) caster sugar
2 eggs
grated rind of 1 orange
100 g (4 oz) self-raising flour
pinch salt
450 g (1 lb) soft fruit
250 ml ($\frac{1}{2}$ pint) double cream

Use strawberries, raspberries, redcurrants or blackcurrants for this, or a mixture of fruit.

Cream the butter and sugar until light and fluffy. Beat the eggs with the orange rind until just mixed together. Sift the flour and salt. Add the eggs to the creamed mixture alternately with the flour so that the mixture does not curdle. Mix well and spread into two greased 18-cm (7-in) sandwich tins. Bake at 190°C (375°F)/Gas 5 for 30 minutes. Cool on a wire rack.

Lightly crush the fruit, reserving some whole fruit for garnishing. Whip the cream to soft peaks, and reserve a few spoonfuls for garnishing. Mix the remaining cream and crushed fruit and sandwich the shortcakes together with this filling. Pipe whirls of cream on the top surface and garnish with whole fruit.

Soft Fruit Steamed Pudding

100 g (4 oz) shredded suet
225 g (8 oz) self-raising flour
pinch salt
675 g (1½ lb) soft fruit
100 g (4 oz) sugar
25 g (1 oz) butter

Stir the suet into the flour with the salt and add just enough cold water to make a firm pastry. Roll out the pastry and use two-thirds to line a greased pudding basin. Prepare the fruit by topping and tailing, or hulling, and put it into the basin with the sugar and butter. Cover with a lid of the remaining pastry, and seal the edges with water. Boil for 2½ hours. Turn out and serve with cream or egg custard or warm honey.

Gooseberries, blackberries or blackcurrants are particularly good for this, but raspberries are also delicious. A mixture of summer fruits can be used, and rhubarb or apples can be mixed with the soft fruit. A mixture of fresh and frozen fruit may be used if this is more convenient.

BLACKBERRIES

Cultivated blackberries have the advantage of being large, glossy and sweet without the multitude of irritating pips which feature so largely in the wild ones. This means they need not be used solely for jams and jellies, but can be used to make many delicious puddings. They are just as good as raspberries served raw with sugar and cream, or used as a filling for a pastry flan or a sponge cake, with whipped cream. Blackberries may be mixed with the last of the summer fruit, but go equally well with autumn apples, pears and quinces. A little rosewater or a couple of rose geranium leaves enhance the flavour if added to blackberry recipes.

Autumn Pudding

350 g (12 oz) blackberries
225 g (8 oz) cooking apples
250 ml (½ pint) dry cider
225 g (8 oz) sugar
5 slices white bread (large loaf)

Put the blackberries into a pan. Peel and core the apples, and slice them into the pan. Add the cider and sugar and simmer until the fruit is soft. Cool the fruit. Remove the crusts from the bread, and use four slices of bread to line a pudding basin. Pour in the fruit mixture and top with the remaining slice of bread. Put a plate on top and a heavy weight on top of the plate. Leave in a cold place for 24 hours. Turn out on to a serving dish, and serve with cream.

Blackberry Betty

450 g (1 lb) cooking apples
350 g (12 oz) blackberries
50 g (2 oz) granulated sugar
50 g (2 oz) butter
175 g (6 oz) fresh white breadcrumbs
50 g (2 oz) soft brown sugar
whipped cream

Peel and core the apples and slice them into a pan. Add the blackberries, reserving a few for decoration, the sugar and 1 tablespoon water. Cover and simmer gently until the fruit is tender, then leave to cool.

Melt the butter in a thick pan, and stir in the breadcrumbs and brown sugar. Turn in the hot butter until the crumbs are well coated with butter and sugar. Arrange a layer of fruit in a serving bowl, then top with a layer of crumbs. Continue in layers, ending with a layer of crumbs. Leave in a cold place for at least 3 hours. Garnish with whipped cream and reserved blackberries.

Blackberry Cream Crowdie

50 g (2 oz) coarse oatmeal
500 ml (1 pint) double cream
50 g (2 oz) caster sugar
1 tablespoon rum
100 g (4 oz) blackberries

Put the oatmeal into a heavy pan and shake over a gentle heat until the oatmeal is crisp. Whip the cream to soft peaks and stir in the toasted oatmeal, sugar, rum and blackberries. Serve at once.

Blackberry Flummery

450 g (1 lb) blackberries
225 g (8 oz) sugar
50 g (1 oz) cornflour
pinch salt
1 teaspoon lemon juice

Put the blackberries and sugar into a pan and just cover with water. Simmer until the fruit is soft and then put through a sieve. Mix the cornflour and salt with 2 tablespoons water, and add to the blackberry purée. Simmer for 5 minutes, stirring very well. Add the lemon juice and turn into a serving bowl. Serve chilled with thin cream.

Blackberry Ice

100 g (4 oz) caster sugar
125 ml (¼ pint) water
2 rose geranium leaves
450 g (1 lb) blackberries

Put the sugar and water into a pan and boil together for 5 minutes. Cool with the rose geranium leaves infusing (if the leaves are not available, use 1 tablespoon rosewater). Wash the blackberries and sieve them. Mix the fruit and syrup and put into a freezer tray. Freeze in the ice-making compartment of the refrigerator at the lowest setting for 1 hour. Put into a cold bowl and beat until soft. Return to the freezer tray, cover with foil and freeze for a further 2 hours.

This recipe may be used for raspberries or strawberries. The rose geranium leaves may be omitted, and a little liqueur (kirsch and rum are particularly appropriate) added instead.

BLACKCURRANTS

Blackcurrants have a high concentration of Vitamin C, and as they also taste delicious, they are invaluable in the kitchen. It is worth growing enough to make jams and syrups for winter use to help ward off colds, as well as using the distinctive flavouring for puddings, pies, ices and fools. For special occasions, a little cassis, the blackcurrant liqueur, helps to strengthen the natural flavour. A pinch of ground cinnamon in pastry used for blackcurrant dishes enhances the flavour.

Blackcurrant Shortcake

450 g (1 lb) blackcurrants
100 g (4 oz) granulated sugar
100 g (4 oz) butter
100 g (4 oz) caster sugar
2 eggs
100 g (4 oz) self-raising flour
pinch salt
250 ml (½ pint) double cream

Strip the currants from their stems and simmer them in 4 tablespoons water with the sugar until tender. Cool completely. Cream together the butter and caster sugar until light and fluffy, and beat in the eggs one by one

77

alternately with the flour sifted with the salt. Put into two greased 17·5-cm (7-in) sandwich tins and bake at 190°C (375°F)/Gas 5 for 25 minutes. Cool on a wire rack. Whip the cream to soft peaks, and sandwich the shortcakes together with the blackcurrants and whipped cream. Dust the top with a little icing sugar before serving.

Blackcurrant Sorbet

450 g (1 lb) blackcurrants
50 g (2 oz) icing sugar
250 ml ($\frac{1}{2}$ pint) natural yoghurt
juice of $\frac{1}{2}$ lemon
15 g ($\frac{1}{2}$ oz) gelatine
4 tablespoons water
2 egg whites

Put the blackcurrants into a pan with 250 ml ($\frac{1}{2}$ pint) water and simmer until the fruit is soft. Put through a sieve and stir in the icing sugar. Cool and mix with the yoghurt and lemon juice.

Put the gelatine into a cup with the water and stand in a pan of hot water until the gelatine is syrupy. Stir this into the blackcurrant purée. Put the mixture into a freezer tray and freeze in the ice-making compartment of the refrigerator at the lowest setting for 1 hour. Whisk the egg whites to stiff peaks. Put the frozen ice into a cold bowl and beat until soft. Fold in the egg whites and return to the freezer tray. Cover with foil and freeze for 2 hours.

GOOSEBERRIES

Gooseberries are easily grown and have the advantage of being used for many dishes while still green and hard, so that they are not as dependent on sunshine as other soft fruit. Large ripe eating gooseberries are delicious whole and on their own, or cut in half and tossed in caster sugar. The hard varieties may be used for pies and puddings and are excellent for jam-making, bottling and freezing. Their sharp flavour is good when used in the same way as apples with rich fatty meat, poultry and fish, but gooseberries are particularly popular in fools and hot puddings. A head of elderflowers cooked with gooseberries gives them a grape-like muscat flavour.

Sweet Gooseberry Sauce

900 g (2 lb) gooseberries
175 g (6 oz) demerara sugar
40 g (1$\frac{1}{2}$ oz) butter

Top and tail the gooseberries and cook them in 250 ml ($\frac{1}{2}$ pint) water with the sugar. When the berries are completely soft, put them through a sieve. Reheat the purée gently, and stir in the butter just before serving. Use with hot or cold puddings, or ices.

Sharp Gooseberry Sauce (for fish)

40 g (1½ oz) butter
20 g (¾ oz) plain flour
225 g (8 oz) gooseberries
salt and pepper
pinch sugar

Melt 25 g (1 oz) butter and stir in the flour. Cook gently until light brown. Stir in 375 ml (¾ pint) water over gentle heat to make a smooth, thin sauce. Top and tail the gooseberries and add to the sauce. Season with salt, pepper and sugar. Simmer until the berries are soft, and put through a sieve. Reheat and add the remaining butter just before serving. This is traditionally served with mackerel, but is equally good with any oily fish, or with rich meat or poultry such as pork or duck.

Gooseberry Amber Pie

225 g (8 oz) shortcrust pastry
675 g (1½ lb) gooseberries
100 g (4 oz) granulated sugar
25 g (1 oz) butter
2 eggs, separated
50 g (2 oz) caster sugar

Line a 20-cm (8-in) pie plate with the pastry. Top and tail the gooseberries and put into a pan with the granulated sugar and 6 tablespoons water. Simmer until the fruit is soft. Cool and then beat in the butter and egg yolks. Put into the pastry case and bake at 190°C (375°F)/Gas 5 for 35 minutes. Whip the egg whites to stiff peaks and fold in the caster sugar. Spread over the fruit and return to the oven for 10 minutes. Serve hot or cold.

Gooseberry Cake

350 g (12 oz) plain flour
½ teaspoon baking powder
½ teaspoon salt
175 g (6 oz) lard
225 g (8 oz) gooseberries
75 g (3 oz) demerara sugar

Keep back 1 teaspoon flour. Sieve the rest of the flour, the baking powder and salt and rub in the lard until the mixture is like breadcrumbs. Add enough cold water to make a stiff paste. Roll out into two 23-cm (9-in) rounds. Put one round on a greased baking sheet. Top and tail the gooseberries and put them on the round of pastry. Sprinkle with the sugar and reserved flour. Top with the second piece of pastry, wetting the edges to seal them, and press them together with a fork. Bake at 200°C (400°F)/Gas 6 for 30 minutes. Cool and dust with a little icing sugar, and serve cold.

Gooseberry Tansy

450 g (1 lb) gooseberries
100 g (4 oz) butter
2 eggs, separated
125 ml (¼ pint) double cream
75 g (3 oz) sugar
25 g (1 oz) butter for frying
a little caster sugar
2 teaspoons lemon juice

Top and tail the gooseberries and put them into a pan with the butter and 4 tablespoons of water. Simmer until the fruit is soft, and then cool. Beat the egg yolks until well mixed. Whip the cream to soft peaks and fold in the yolks. Stir in the cool gooseberries and add the granulated sugar. Whisk the egg whites to stiff peaks and fold into the mixture. Melt the butter in an omelette pan and pour in the gooseberry mixture. Cook gently for 5 minutes until the mixture sets and is puffed up. Put on to a hot serving dish and sprinkle with caster sugar and lemon juice.

Loganberries

Loganberries are similar to raspberries but have the slightly acid flavour of mulberries, and they may be used for old-fashioned mulberry recipes. They are better cooked than raw, and can be used for any raspberry, blackberry or mulberry dishes. Their colour is very rich and they can be mixed with other summer fruit such as strawberries, gooseberries and raspberries to give a slightly sharp flavour and ruby colouring to puddings and jams.

Loganberry Charlotte

350 g (12 oz) loganberries
3 cooking apples

50 g (2 oz) butter
pinch cinnamon
100 g (4 oz) soft white breadcrumbs
100 g (4 oz) demerara sugar

Clean the loganberries if necessary. Peel and core the apples and cut them into slices. Melt the butter in a thick pan. Mix the cinnamon, breadcrumbs and sugar and toss in the butter until well coated. Put a thin layer of the crumbs on the bottom of a greased ovenware dish and cover with a layer of apple slices. Sprinkle with crumbs, then a layer of loganberries. Continue in these layers, finishing with a thick layer of crumbs. Bake at 170°C (325°F)/Gas 3 for 1 hour.

Serve with cream or egg custard.

Loganberry Sponge

50 g (2 oz) butter
175 g (6 oz) caster sugar
2 eggs
100 g (4 oz) self-raising flour
350 g (12 oz) loganberries
1 large eating apple

Cream the butter and sugar until light and fluffy. Beat the eggs lightly with a fork and add them to the creamed mixture alternately with the flour. Add the loganberries. Peel, core and slice the apple, and fold the slices into the mixture. Turn into a greased pudding basin and cover with foil. Put into a pan of boiling water and boil for 1½ hours. Turn out and serve with cream or egg custard.

If preferred, put the mixture into a greased ovenware dish and bake at 180°C (350°F)/Gas 4 for 1 hour.

RASPBERRIES

The fresh flavour of raw raspberries is perfect with sugar and cream, but for a special occasion, a sprinkling of claret, sauternes or champagne enhances the flavour. A little kirsch is also a popular accompaniment to raspberry dishes, or to a mixture of summer fruits such as raspberries and redcurrants, or raspberries and strawberries. These berries also go very well with peaches (raspberry sauce with fresh peaches is a classic pudding), and with a mixture of blackcurrants and eating gooseberries. As with blackcurrants, a pinch of ground cinnamon enhances the flavour, and a pinch of ground coffee in the pastry for raspberry dishes is an exciting addition.

Raspberry Cream

450 g (1 lb) raspberries
75 g (3 oz) caster sugar
250 ml (½ pint) double cream
2 egg whites

Put the raspberries into a bowl and sprinkle with the sugar. Leave for 1 hour, and then put them through a sieve. Whip the cream to soft peaks and fold in the raspberry purée. Whisk the egg whites to stiff peaks, and fold them lightly into the purée. Put into a serving bowl or individual glasses and chill. Serve with small sweet biscuits.

Raspberry Honey Ice

450 g (1 lb) raspberries
125 ml (¼ pint) double cream
125 ml (¼ pint) natural yoghurt
225 g (8 oz) clear honey
2 tablespoons lemon juice
pinch salt
4 egg whites

Sieve the raspberries. Whip the cream to soft peaks and mix with the yoghurt, honey, lemon juice, salt and raspberry purée. Put into a freezer tray and freeze in the ice-making compartment of the refrigerator, at its lowest setting, for 1 hour. Put into a cold bowl and beat until soft. Whisk the egg whites to stiff peaks and fold them into the fruit mixture. Return to the freezer tray, cover with foil and freeze for 2 hours.

Raspberry Puff

450 g (1 lb) raspberries
125 ml (¼ pint) soured cream
2 eggs
25 g (1 oz) caster sugar
15 g (½ oz) plain flour

Put the raspberries into an ovenware dish and cover with a lid or piece of foil. Bake at 180°C (350°F)/Gas 4 for 15 minutes. Beat the cream with a fork and gradually work in the eggs, sugar and flour. Pour over the fruit. Bake uncovered at 170°C (325°F)/Gas 3 for 20 minutes. Serve very hot.

Raspberry Salad (for poultry)

225 g (8 oz) raspberries

4 tablespoons oil
2 tablespoons lemon juice
pinch sugar
lettuce leaves

Put the raspberries into a bowl and cover with the mixed oil, lemon juice
and sugar. Leave to stand for 30 minutes. Put lettuce leaves on individual
plates and arrange raspberries in a mound on each. Serve with roast
chicken or duck.

REDCURRANTS

Redcurrants are very good served raw with a sprinkling of sugar, but are
less successful when stewed into a mass of pips and liquid. They blend very
well with raspberries for a two-fruit combination, and also go well in a
mixed bowl of summer fruit. Redcurrant juice gives excellent flavour and
setting quality to low-pectin fruit jams such as strawberry, while
redcurrant jelly is essential to the enjoyment of mutton, veal, hare and
venison.

Redcurrant Pieces

150 g (5 oz) butter
225 g (8 oz) caster sugar
2 eggs, separated
175 g (6 oz) plain flour
1 teaspoon grated lemon rind
350 g (12 oz) redcurrants

Cream the butter with 50 g (2 oz) sugar until light and fluffy. Beat in the egg
yolks and fold in the flour and lemon rind to make a stiff mixture. Spread on
a greased and floured Swiss roll tin. Bake at 190°C (375°F)/Gas 5 for 20
minutes until golden brown. Leave on the tin and cool slightly. Remove the
redcurrants from their strings and spread on to the cake. Whisk the egg
whites to stiff peaks and then whisk in 50 g (2 oz) sugar. Continue whisking
until the mixture is smooth and shiny and fold in 75 g (3 oz) sugar. Pile the
mixture on to the fruit and sprinkle with the remaining sugar. Bake at
180°C (350°F)/Gas 4 for 30 minutes. When it is done, the meringue
topping will sound hollow if gently tapped. Cool and cut in slices before
removing from the baking tin.

STRAWBERRIES

Most of us enjoy strawberries served plainly with sugar and cream. The

83

small alpine strawberry is better without cream. People have been known to eat freshly-gathered strawberries with a pinch of salt, or a shake of pepper, but a sprinkling of orange juice, claret or champagne is more traditional. Port is also good with this fruit. Strawberries blend well with all the other summer fruits, but are seldom served cooked. They are excellent used as a filling for flans, shortcakes and spongecakes, combined with whipped cream and the addition of a little grated orange rind. The strawberry changes completely in flavour and texture when cooked or preserved, but makes one of the most popular jams. Strawberry purée freezes well, but whole strawberries are not good for either freezing or bottling.

Hot Strawberry Compote

450 g (1 lb) strawberries
175 g (6 oz) sugar
pinch cinnamon
125 ml (¼ pint) red wine
1 tablespoon honey
2 teaspoons lemon juice

Hull the strawberries and put them into an ovenware dish with the sugar and cinnamon. Cover with a lid or some foil and cook at 170°C (325°F)/Gas 3 for 30 minutes. Drain off the syrup from the strawberries and mix it with the wine. Pour this over the fruit and continue cooking for 15 minutes. Stir in the honey and lemon juice, and serve hot with thick cream.

Storing, Drying, Bottling and Freezing

Many root and green vegetables will stay happily in the ground, but it is often more convenient to harvest vegetables and store them by clamping, drying or freezing. Fruits may be bottled or frozen. Home canning is now rarely practised and it is difficult to find the equipment.

DRY STORAGE

A frostproof shed, cellar or attic can be used for many types of root vegetables and for fruit, and no equipment is necessary, except for a few old boxes and some straw.

Apples and Pears The apples which ripen latest store best. Do not put apples into store immediately after picking, but let them cool and sweat in an airy place before storing. Store in a dark, cool, slightly moist place. Keep different varieties separately and stack them in boxes which have a space between (tomato boxes are ideal as they can be divided by the upstanding corners). Store special eating apples by wrapping them individually in sheets of newspaper before packing into boxes. Pears may be kept in the same way but should be inspected frequently, as they ripen very suddenly. Remove unsound fruit regularly.

Beetroot Cover with straw, or put into a box covered with sand.

Carrots Lift by mid-November and store in boxes raised above ground level on bricks in a cool shed.

Marrows and Pumpkins Store in a cool dry place away from frost. Marrows may also be cut when ripe, but not old, with plenty of stalk on them. Seal the stalk end with candle wax. Tie a piece of tape, which will not cut the skin, round each end of the marrow, and hang in a cool dry place.

Onions Tie in bunches or plait in strings and hang in an airy place.

Parsnips Store under straw in a cool shed.

Potatoes Store in hessian or paper sacks indoors.

Turnips Store in a heap under straw or sand in a cool shed.

CLAMPING

When indoor storage space is scarce, root crops may be stored in outdoor clamps which will take large quantities of vegetables. See that the ground is dry, and only store roots that have grown to maturity and are thoroughly dry. Pile the roots in a ridge and cover them with a 12·5-cm (5-in) layer of dry straw which is completely clean. Put a 15-cm (6-in) layer of sifted soil over the whole clamp, pressing it down firmly. A small vent must be made at the top with either a few strands of straw or a small pipe. Dig a trench around the sides of the clamp for drainage, and rake or fork in some cinders or stones. The trench should be about 15 cm (6 in) below the level of the ground on which the vegetables are standing. Whenever the clamp is opened, it should be sealed again with more straw and soil. The clamp should not be opened in wet or frosty weather.

SALTING

Runner beans can be salted for storage in a large earthenware jar or in a glass preserving jar. Use block cooking salt, not table salt, for this preservation method.

Pick the beans when young and tender and preserve them while very fresh. Wash the beans, dry them in a cloth and slice as for cooking. Put a layer of salt in the container, then beans. Continue in layers, finishing with salt. Press well down and cover for a few days until the beans have sunk down in the container. Top up with more beans and salt and then exclude

86

the air from the container with an airtight lid or cork. Be liberal with the salt, or the beans will be slimy and useless. About 450 g (1 lb) salt will be needed for each 1·35 kg (3 lb) beans.

Wash the beans very thoroughly in plenty of fresh cold water before use, and leave them to soak for 2 hours in cold water. Do not soak them overnight or they will become tough. Cook in boiling water as usual.

Drying

Drying needs no special equipment, but food must be dried slowly because it is important that it does *dry*, not scorch or cook.

Peas and beans, onions and leeks, mushrooms, apples, pears and plums can all be dried in a very low oven, on the slatted shelves of an airing cupboard, or on a shelf over a solid fuel cooker. In a cupboard or over a cooker, the food should be spread out on a wire cake rack and covered lightly with muslin to prevent dust contamination. There should be a constant gentle heat with a current of air to carry away moisture, so that a cupboard or oven door must be left slightly open. The ideal heat for drying is no more than 70°C (150°F)/Gas $\frac{1}{4}$. All dried foods must be completely cold before being packed into jars or boxes with tightly-fitting lids. They should be stored in a dry, airy, dark place if possible, as light causes colour changes. Any sign of mould indicates that the food was not properly dried, or that the storage place is warm and damp. Do not use dried foods if they seem musty or sour-smelling.

Apples Use firm, juicy, crisp apples which are not over-ripe. Peel and core them, and cut them into 0·5-cm ($\frac{1}{4}$-in) rings. Put them in a solution of 25 g (1 oz) salt to 2 litres (4 pints) water for 10 minutes. Drain them and thread on thin sticks, and rest the sticks on oven racks so that the apple rings do not touch each other. Dry until the apples are like dry chamois leather but pliable. Cool thoroughly and pack in jars. Soak overnight before using and cook in soaking water.

Mushrooms Use very fresh, open mushrooms for drying and remove the stems. Wipe with a damp cloth, and thread the mushrooms on a fine string with a knot between each to prevent them touching. Hang them in oven from the oven rack, or in a warm airy place which is not steamy, and dry as for other vegetables. When ready for storing, the mushrooms will be like dry chamois leather. Store in jars. Soak in cold water for a few minutes before frying or grilling, or add to casseroles and soups while still dry.

Onions and Leeks Peel medium-sized onions and cut them into slices about 0·5 cm ($\frac{1}{4}$ in) thick. Separate the slices into rings, and use the inner rings for immediate cooking as they are too small for drying. Put the larger rings into fast boiling water for 30 seconds, drain in a colander and chill in cold water. Drain and dry with kitchen paper. Spread them on a rack and dry in the oven. When the rings are crisp and dry, cool and store in jars or boxes. **Leeks** should be well cleaned and cut in strips before blanching for 15 seconds and drying as for onions. Soak onions and leeks for 30 minutes in cold water before using.

Pears Pears should be firm but ripe, and after peeling they should be cut in halves and the cores removed. Put into salt water as for apples, but for 5 minutes only. Drain and arrange on a wire cake rack covered with muslin, dry in a warm oven until the pears are rubbery but not coloured, and store. Soak overnight before using and cook in soaking water.

Peas and Beans Leave *marrowfat peas* and *haricot beans* on the plants until dry and withered. Pull up the plants and hang them in an airy shed. Shell the peas and beans and spread them on a tray in a warm place. When they are completely hard and dry, store in an airtight container in a cool dark place. Soak overnight in cold water before using.

Plums Use firm ripe purple plums and dry them whole or in halves with the stones removed. Spread them on a wire rack covered with muslin, with the cut side uppermost to prevent juice running out. The temperature for drying plums should be low so that the pulp dries without the skins hardening too quickly. The fruit is ready when it can be squeezed without any moisture coming out. Cool thoroughly before packing. Soak overnight before using and cook in soaking water.

BOTTLING

There are two main methods of bottling fruit: sterilisation in a water-bath or heating in a moderate oven. (It is not advisable to bottle vegetables unless you use a pressure cooker, and complete accuracy is required.)

Packing the Fruit

Pack *soft* fruit in the bottles as tightly as possible without bruising, and add syrup or water every four layers as packing continues. Pack *hard* fruit tightly, and fill with syrup or water after packing, giving the bottles a sharp jerk to remove air bubbles. A long-handled wooden spoon is best to pack with. For *tomatoes*, use brine made from 15 g ($\frac{1}{2}$ oz) salt to 875 ml ($1\frac{3}{4}$ pints) water. For *apples*, use a syrup made from 225 g (8 oz) sugar to 500 ml (1 pint) water; *soft fruit and pears* can be bottled in heavy syrup using 350 g

(12 oz) sugar to 500 ml (1 pint) water. To make the syrup, dissolve the sugar in half the water, boil for 2 minutes, then add remaining water and strain. Use when cold.

Water-bath Method

Use screw-band bottles, either with glass lids and rubber rings, or with a metal lid fitted with a rubber ring and a screw-band. If jars with glass lids are used, new rubber rings must always be used to ensure a satisfactory seal.

A large container is needed for holding the water on the stove. The container must be deep enough to hold enough water to cover the bottles completely. A wire or wooden rack, or a thick pad of newspaper, must be used to form a false bottom to the pan, so that bottles do not come in direct contact with heat. A thermometer is essential for this method. After packing firmly, cover the fruit with cold syrup (or tomatoes with brine), put the lid on, secure it, and loosen the screw-band a quarter of a turn. The bottles should then be completely covered with cold water, and the pan covered with a lid or board. Bring the water slowly to the boil, allowing 1 hour for it to rise to 55°C (130°F). Raise the water to the required temperature, according to the fruit, in 30 minutes, and process for the length of time required (see page 90). Remove the jars from the water and tighten the screw-bands.

Oven Method

Pack in the same way as for the water-bath method. Preheat the oven to 150°C (300°F)/Gas 2. Pour boiling syrup or brine on the fruit or tomatoes, leaving 2·5 cm (1 in) headspace. Put the lids on top, but not the screw-bands. Put the bottles on a baking tray thickly lined with newspaper, and do not let the bottles touch each other. Place them in the centre of the oven, process for the length of time shown on page 90, and then remove from the oven and screw on the bands.

Testing the Seal

When the screw-bands have been tightened after processing, the jars should be left for 24 hours. Then take off the bands, and lift the bottles carefully by the lids. If they are secure, the seal is complete. If the seal is not complete, the fruit can be re-processed (though it may become rather soft) or it can be used at once.

FRUIT	Water-bath temperature	Time maintained (minutes)	Oven method 150°C (300°F)/ Gas 2 (minutes)
Apples	74°C (165°F)	10	40
Blackberries	,,	,,	,,
Gooseberries	,,	,,	,,
Raspberries	,,	,,	,,
Rhubarb	,,	,,	,,
Strawberries	,,	,,	,,
Apricots	83°C (180°F)	15	50
Cherries	,,	,,	,,
Currants	,,	,,	,,
Damsons	,,	,,	,,
Greengages	,,	,,	,,
Peaches	,,	,,	,,
Plums	,,	,,	,,
Pears	88°C (190°F)	30	70
Tomatoes in brine	,,	,,	,,

FREEZING

Freezing is the best way of preserving most fruit and vegetables because it retains flavour, colour and texture, and nutritive value. Only freeze young tender vegetables and fresh ripe fruit, and process immediately after harvesting. Harvest regularly each day and freeze produce at once, rather than waiting until a large batch is ready, by which time some vegetables will be tough and stringy, and fruit will be over-ripe. It is recommended that no more than 1·35 kg (3 lb) of fresh produce should be frozen for each 28·3 litres (cubic foot) of freezer space at any one time. It takes about 6 hours to freeze garden produce hard, so it is possible to freeze two batches in one day.

Vegetables

Prepare vegetables only just before freezing. Make plenty of extra ice and store it in the freezer during the peak freezing season, as a great deal is needed during preparation. Put on the fast-freeze switch 2–3 hours before freezing.

Wash vegetables thoroughly in cold water, grade them into sizes or cut them if necessary. It is possible to freeze unblanched vegetables for storage up to 3 months, but they quickly lose colour, flavour and nutritive value, and it is a pity to spoil top-quality garden produce by neglecting correct preparation. It is essential to blanch vegetables if you are going to freeze them for more than 3 months. Over-blanching results in flabby, colourless vegetables, and under-blanching means a colour change and loss of nutritive value. Put 4·5 litres (8 pints) water into a saucepan, and put a blanching basket in the pan. Bring the water to the boil and add the vegetables. Only blanch 450 g (1 lb) vegetables at a time. Cover with a lid, and bring the water back to the boil quickly. Start timing as soon as it boils, and immediately the time is up (see pp. 93–96), take out the blanching basket. Tip the vegetables into a colander standing in a bowl of cold water and ice cubes. (Running water from a tap is not cold enough to chill vegetables properly.) Chill for the same length of time as the vegetables were blanched. Drain thoroughly and open-freeze or pack at once. Put bags in single layers in the fast-freeze compartment or, in an older freezer, see that each bag touches the sides or bottom of the freezer.

Many vegetables can be open-frozen before they are stored in the freezer, so that they are frozen individually and will flow freely when packed. To do this, use a baking sheet or tray, or a polythene box lid, or a special fast-freeze tray with foil lining. Spread out the vegetables in a single layer and freeze till hard. Pack in bags or rigid containers, excluding air.

Most vegetables keep well for 12 months in the freezer, but about 9 months is usually the maximum required before new produce is in season again. Salad vegetables which contain a lot of water, such as lettuce and radishes, are not suitable for freezing. A few items such as celery, chicory and tomatoes can be frozen, but are then only useful for cooking and cannot be eaten raw after freezing. If freezer space is short, freeze the luxury vegetable produce such as asparagus and artichokes, and peas, beans and courgettes.

Fruit

Fruit does not change its character appreciably during freezing, and frozen fruit, unlike bottled fruit, will taste freshly picked. Freeze only top-quality fruit which is perfectly ripe but not over-ripe. Freeze immediately after picking and work with small quantities which can be prepared quickly.

Wash fruit in ice-chilled water to firm it before processing so that no juice is lost. Extract any stems or stones carefully to avoid juice loss. Pack fruit in a variety of ways for best results. An unsweetened dry pack is very satisfactory, as the fruit can then be used in many different ways. A sweetened dry pack is good for juicy fruits, but the sugar tends to draw out juice and results in mushiness in thawing, as well as making the fruit too sweet for some people's taste and for many recipes. Fruit in syrup is useful for speedy service but is limited in use for making up into recipes. Fruit purées take up little space in the freezer and are useful for making ices, mousses and fools later.

Unsweetened Dry Pack Dry fruit after washing and pack in bags or rigid containers. If liked, open-freeze fruit before packing. Any light-coloured fruit which discolours badly should not be packed without sugar, as this helps to retard the action of the enzymes which cause darkening.

Sweetened Dry Pack Mix the required sugar (see pages 96–97) with the fruit before packing, or arrange layers of fruit and sugar in a rigid pack, starting with fruit and ending with a sugar layer.

Syrup Pack Syrup for freezing fruit should be made with white sugar and water. Brown sugar and honey affect the colour and flavour of fruit. The sugar should be dissolved in boiling water and cooled completely before use. A little lemon juice or citric or abscorbic acid should be added for apples, peaches and pears, which discolour easily. Syrups are usually prepared in three strengths:

Light syrup: 225 g (8 oz) sugar to 500 ml (1 pint) water
Medium syrup: 350 g (12 oz) sugar to 500 ml (1 pint) water
Heavy syrup: 450 g (1 lb) sugar to 500 ml (1 pint) water

Fruit should be packed into rigid containers and covered with syrup, allowing 1 cm ($\frac{1}{2}$ in) headspace for expansion. For light-coloured fruit, this space should be filled with crumpled foil or freezer paper to prevent fruit rising above the syrup and discolouring on contact with the air.

Fruit purée may be either raw or cooked, and should be sweetened to taste before freezing.

Apples, peaches and pears are particularly subject to darkening during preparation, storage and thawing. Vitamin C, in the form of lemon juice, citric or ascorbic acid, helps to prevent this, and can be added to dry sugar packs or syrup. Fruit purée darkens easily because of the amount of air forced through the sieve. Fruit keeps well for 12 months in the freezer, but fruit purée may lose some quality after 4 months.

Only thaw fruit in usable quantities as it quickly darkens and loses flavour if left to stand once thawed. If possible, thaw fruit in the refrigerator, allowing 6 hours for 450 g (1 lb) fruit. Unsweetened packs take longer to thaw than sweetened ones, and dry sugar packs thaw most quickly. Keep fruit covered until the moment you want to use it if it is likely to discolour (e.g. peaches and apricots). Fruit is best served when just thawed and still frosty. Partly thawed fruit can be put into pies or puddings, or can be cooked in hot syrup. If frozen unsweetened fruit is used for jam, allow 10% more fruit than called for in a standard recipe, as there is slight pectin loss in the freezing process.

Vegetables

Artichokes (Globe) Trim the outer leaves and stalks and wash thoroughly, removing the hairy 'chokes'. Blanch 7 minutes, with 1 tablespoon lemon juice in the water. Cool and drain well and pack in rigid containers. If preferred, remove all leaves and blanch hearts for 5 minutes, then pack them in bags or rigid containers.

Artichokes (Jerusalem) Peel and cut into pieces. Soften slightly in butter and cook in chicken stock. Sieve and freeze as purée in rigid containers.

Asparagus Wash well and remove woody ends and small scales. Cut asparagus into 15-cm (6-in) lengths, and grade according to thickness. Do not tie into bundles, but blanch each size separately. Allow 2 minutes for small spears, 3 for medium, and 4 for large. Cool immediately and drain well. Pack in plastic boxes, in sizes or mixed bundles.

Aubergines Use tender, mature, medium-sized aubergines. Cut the vegetable, unpeeled, into 2·5-cm (1-in) slices. Blanch 4 minutes, cool, drain and pack in layers separated by clingfilm or freezer paper in rigid containers.

Beans (Broad) Use young small beans with tender skins. Remove from pods and blanch 1½ minutes. Open-freeze before packing in bags.

Beans (Dwarf) Use young tender beans about the thickness of a bootlace. Top and tail. Freeze small beans whole, or cut into 2·5-cm (1-in) pieces. Blanch 3 minutes (whole) or 2 minutes (cut). Cool and pack in bags.

Beans (Runner) Use young beans, no longer than 17·5 cm (7 in). Do not shred finely, but string them and slice thickly in chunks. Blanch 2 minutes, cool and pack in bags.

Beetroot Use small young beet no more than 7·5 cm (3 in) in diameter. Cook completely, cool quickly and rub off skins. Pack whole, or in slices or dice.

Broccoli and Calabrese Use compact heads with tender stalks not more than 2·5 cm (1 in) thick. Trim off woody stems and outer leaves. Wash well in salted water for 30 minutes, and rinse in clean water. Blanch 3 minutes (thin stems), 4 minutes (medium stems), or 5 minutes (thick stems). Cool and pack in rigid containers, alternating heads.

Brussels Sprouts Use small compact sprouts and remove discoloured leaves. Grade for size and blanch 3 minutes (small) or 4 minutes (medium). Cool, open-freeze and pack in bags.

Cabbage Shred finely and blanch $1\frac{1}{2}$ minutes. Pack in rigid containers.

Carrots Use small young carrots, remove tops, wash and scrape well. Leave small ones whole, but slice larger carrots. Blanch 3 minutes (whole) or 2 minutes (sliced), cool, drain and pack in bags.

Cauliflower Use firm heads with close white curds. Freeze very small heads whole, break larger heads into sprigs. Wash thoroughly. Blanch 3 minutes, with the juice of 1 lemon in the blanching water. Cool and pack in bags.

Celeriac Cut into slices and blanch 3 minutes, adding a little lemon juice to the water. Cool and pack in bags. If preferred, cook celeriac in a little water and freeze it as a purée. Celeriac cannot be used in salads after freezing.

Celery Use tender, crisp stalks and remove strings. Wash well, cut into 2·5-cm (1-in) lengths and blanch 3 minutes. Cool and drain and pack dry in bags. If preferred, pack in some of the blanching liquid which can be used for later cooking. Leave 1 cm ($\frac{1}{2}$ in) headspace in rigid containers. Celery cannot be used raw after freezing, but is useful to serve as a vegetable, or to add to stews and soups.

Chicory Use compact heads with yellow tips. Trim stalks and remove any bruised outside leaves. Put the juice of 1 lemon in the water, and blanch 2 minutes. Cool and drain very thoroughly before packing in rigid containers. Chicory cannot be used for salads after freezing.

Herbs Pick soft-leaved herbs (basil, chervil, chives, mint, parsley, tarragon) when young. Wash and pack in sprigs in bags. If preferred, chop herbs finely and pack into ice-cube trays with a spoonful of water. Freeze and transfer the frozen cubes to bags for storage. This method is particularly satisfactory for mint and parsley. Frozen herbs become limp on thawing and are not suitable to use as sprigs for garnishing.

Kale Use young, tender, lightly curled kale, and discard discoloured or tough leaves. Wash very well and pull leaves from stems. Blanch 1 minute and drain well after cooling. If liked, chop leaves for easier packing in bags, but do this after blanching.

94

Leeks Use young even-sized leeks, remove coarse outer leaves and trim off green tops. Wash in cold running water. Cut larger leeks into 1-cm (½-in) rings, but leave small ones whole. Blanch 3 minutes (whole), 2 minutes (sliced). Pack in rigid containers or in bags, but overwrap bags as leeks smell strongly.

Marrows and Courgettes Large older marrows are best cooked and frozen as purée. Cut tender young courgettes, or very small marrows into 0·5-cm (¼-in) slices without peeling. Blanch 1 minute, or toss slices in hot butter until tender. Open-freeze blanched slices and pack in bags. Pack fried slices in rigid containers.

Mushrooms Grade mushrooms for size, and wipe them, but do not peel. Pack in bags, packing stalks separately if liked. Small button mushrooms can be cooked in butter (75 g (3 oz) butter to 450 g (1 lb) mushrooms) for 5 minutes, then packed in rigid containers for freezing.

Onions Peel small onions and leave them whole, but peel and chop larger ones. Blanch 3 minutes (whole), 2 minutes (chopped), cool and drain and pack in bags, but overwrap bags as onions smell strongly.

Parsnips Old parsnips are best cooked and frozen as purée. Young parsnips should be peeled and cut into thin strips or dice. Blanch 2 minutes, cool, drain and pack in bags.

Peas Use young, tender sweet peas. Blanch 1 minute and pack in bags. If preferred, peas may be open-frozen before packing. Sugar peas (mange tout) should be frozen while the pods are still flat. Top, tail and string them and blanch 2 minutes. Cool, drain and pack in bags.

Peppers Use firm, plump, glossy peppers. Wash and dry them, cut off stems, and remove seeds and membranes. Cut in halves, slices or dice. Blanch 3 minutes (halves), 2 minutes (slices or dice), cool, drain and pack in bags.

Potatoes Do not freeze potatoes blanched in water, or plainly boiled old potatoes. Cooked jacket potatoes, roast, creamed and duchesse potatoes, and potato croquettes may be frozen. *Chips* must not be frozen raw or boiled in water, but should be fried in clean fat until soft but not coloured before draining, cooling and packing in bags. *New potatoes* are best scraped, graded for size, and slightly undercooked. Drain and toss in butter and pack in boil-in-bags (for serving, put the whole bag in boiling water, remove from heat and leave 10 minutes).

Spinach Use young tender leaves without heavy ribs. Strip leaves from stems, and remove bruised or discoloured leaves. Wash very well and blanch 2 minutes, shaking the blanching basket so the leaves do not mat together. Cool quickly and press out excess moisture. Pack in bags or rigid containers. Do not add any water during reheating.

Squashes and Pumpkins Cook the flesh in very little water until soft. Mash well and freeze as purée in rigid containers.

Tomatoes Tomatoes cannot be used for salads after freezing as they become soft, but they are very useful for cooking. Wipe whole tomatoes, grade for size and freeze in bags (the skins will drop off when thawed). If preferred, cut tomatoes in half and open-freeze before packing (these halves are useful for grilling or frying). Tomatoes may also be skinned, cored and simmered in their own juice before sieving and freezing as purée.

Turnips and Swedes Peel and cut in dice and blanch $2\frac{1}{2}$ minutes. Cool, drain and pack in bags. It may be more convenient to cook turnips and swedes completely, sieve them and freeze them as purée, as they are so often eaten in that form.

Fruit

Apples Peel, core and drop in cold water. Cut in slices and pack in bags or rigid containers. Use dry sugar pack (225 g (8 oz) sugar to 900 g (2 lb) fruit) or medium syrup. 'Fluffy' cooking apples are better cooked, sweetened and frozen as purée.

Apricots Wash firm ripe fruit, cut in halves and take out stones. Drop in boiling water for 30 seconds and chill in cold water. Pack at once in rigid containers. Use dry sugar pack (225 g (8 oz) sugar to 900 g (2 lb) fruit) or medium syrup adding $\frac{1}{4}$ teaspoon ascorbic acid.

Blackberries Use fully-ripe, dark glossy berries. Open-freeze and pack unsweetened in bags. If preferred, use dry sugar pack (225 g (8 oz) sugar to 900 g (2 lb) fruit) or heavy syrup, or pack as sweetened purée.

Cherries Use sweet or sour varieties and leave in ice-cold water for 1 hour before freezing. Dry cherries and remove stones. Pack in rigid containers. Use dry sugar pack (225 g (8 oz) sugar to 900 g (2 lb) fruit), medium syrup (sweet fruit) or heavy syrup (sour fruit).

Currants Strip stems from currants and wash fruit in ice-cold water. Dry well and pack in bags or rigid containers. Use unsweetened pack, dry sugar pack (450 g (1 lb) sugar to 900 g (2 lb) fruit), or medium syrup. Black-currants may be cooked, sweetened and packed as purée.

Figs Wash in ice-cold water and remove stems without bruising. Pack peeled or unpeeled in dry unsweetened pack, or in light syrup.

Gooseberries Wash in ice-cold water and dry. Pack in bags or rigid containers, with dry unsweetened pack or medium syrup. Alternatively, freeze gooseberries as a cooked, sweetened purée.

Grapes Peel, halve, and remove seeds, then pack in light syrup in rigid containers.

Peaches Peel, halve and remove stones, and brush fruit with lemon juice. Work quickly as this fruit discolours easily. Pack in halves or slices in medium syrup with $\frac{1}{4}$ teaspoon ascorbic acid.

Pears Use strongly-flavoured ripe pears. Peel and quarter fruit and remove cores. Dip pieces in lemon juice and poach in light syrup for $1\frac{1}{2}$ minutes. Drain pears, cool, and pack in cold syrup in rigid containers.

Plums Wash in ice-cold water, dry well and remove stones. Whole raw plums may be packed unsweetened in bags. If preferred, use dry sugar pack for halved plums (225 g (8 oz) sugar to 900 g (2 lb) fruit) or medium syrup.

Raspberries and Loganberries Wash in ice-cold water and drain well. Open-freeze and pack unsweetened in bags. If preferred, use dry sugar pack (225 g (8 oz) sugar to 900 g (2 lb) fruit) or light syrup. Fresh berries may be sieved, sweetened and frozen as purée.

Rhubarb Use young pink sticks, and freeze either raw or cooked. Wash, trim and cut in lengths. Pack long sticks in foil or polythene bags, or cut in 2·5-cm (1-in) lengths and pack unsweetened in bags. If preferred, pack in medium syrup in rigid containers, or cook, sweeten and pack as purée.

Strawberries Remove hulls, wash in ice-cold water and dry well. Open-freeze and pack unsweetened in polythene bags. If preferred, pack in medium syrup, or as raw sweetened purée.

Pickles and Chutneys

A wide variety of surplus fruit and vegetables can be used for spicy pickles and chutneys which are useful to keep in the store cupboard to accompany simple meals of meat, fish or cheese, or to use in sandwiches. It is a good idea to make these vinegar-based preserves in the late summer and autumn when small quantities of surplus produce may be mixed together. The recipes in this chapter serve as a guideline, but it is possible to vary the solid ingredients according to what is available, keeping to the basic cooking method and proportions of vinegar, sugar, spice and dried fruit.

Avoid any pickling equipment which could give a metallic flavour—the best pans to use are large and thick, and made of aluminium or unchipped enamel. When other equipment is needed, use nylon or hair sieves, stainless steel knives and wooden spoons. For storing the pickles, use clean, dry warm jars with screwtops or plastic lids. If the lids are made of metal, they must be lined with ceresin discs, which are vinegar-proof. Jars saved from bought pickles and instant coffee jars are both ideal to use for vinegar-based pickles. The pickles should never be covered with jam-pot paper covers or brown paper as these allow the contents to dry out.

Although pickles are usually made from surplus produce, it is important that the vegetables and fruit should be fresh and just ripe. Many vegetables have to be covered in dry salt or soaked in brine before pickling (see individual recipes), and the salt to use is cooking or block salt, as table salt

Apple and tomatoe Chutney

3 lbs cooking apples
3 lbs tomatoes Red or green
1 lb sugar
2 tea spoon ginger
1 tea spoon spices
1 lb onions
3/4 lb sultanas
1 tea spoon salt
1 pint malt vinegar

Peel, core and slice apples chop onions small, cut tomatoes into chunky pieces. Place in bowl & cover with venegar leave for 24 hours.

Place in pan, add sultanas, sugar spices & salt. Bring to the boil, keep at simmering until all ingredients are tender & mixture thickens. Stir frequently. Pour into hot jars & cover.

Apple Chutney

6 lbs apples
2 lbs sultanas
3/4 lbs Preserved ginger
3 Pts vinegar
3 1/2 lbs sugar
1 oz salt
1 tea spoon spice

Peel, core and chop apples into small
pieces chop up sultanas & ginger, Mix
vinegar, sugar, salt + spice together
+ bring to the boil, add apples +
simmer for 10 minutes, add the
ginger + sultanas simmer until
the mixture becomes fairly
thick, & pour into jars.

contains a chemical which is not satisfactory for pickling. Vinegar is another essential for pickling. Malt vinegar is acceptable for most pickles and chutneys, but spiced fruits and clear pickles are better made with white vinegar, while cider and wine vinegars give the best flavour. Cold vinegar will give a crisp pickle (e.g. red cabbage), whereas hot vinegar gives a soft pickle (e.g. beetroot). Whole spices can be purchased from chemists and grocers, and are best tied into a small piece of muslin or an old clean handkerchief, suspended in the cooking pan. Ground spices can be used in chutney or mustard pickles, but will make clear pickles cloudy. Brown or white sugar may be used; the brown varieties give a rich flavour and colour, but they are not as suitable when a pale clear syrup is required.

Pickles and chutneys need time to mature to taste at their best. Crisp pickles may be eaten after two or three weeks, but will be at their best after about 3 months. Sweet pickles, mustard pickles and chutneys can be eaten after 3 months, but will be better after 6 months. All kinds of pickles are best stored in a cool, dry, dark place.

Pickled Beetroot

8 medium-sized beetroot
7 g ($\frac{1}{4}$ oz) black peppercorns
25 g (1 oz) grated horseradish
7 g ($\frac{1}{4}$ oz) whole allspice
1 teaspoon salt
1 litre (2 pints) vinegar

Clean the beetroot without breaking the skin. Put on a baking sheet and bake at 160°C (325°F)/Gas 3 for 1$\frac{1}{2}$ hours. (If preferred, the beetroot may be boiled until tender, but the flavour is better when the vegetable is baked.) Cool the beetroot, skin and cut in slices, and put into jars. Put all the remaining ingredients into a saucepan and bring to the boil. Boil for 2 minutes and then cool. Pour over the beetroot and cover tightly.

Pickled Cabbage

1 large firm red cabbage
cooking salt
cayenne pepper
vinegar

Cut the cabbage in quarters and take out the stalk. Slice the cabbage very thinly and put it on a large flat dish. Sprinkle with salt and leave overnight. Next day, stir well to mix the salt and liquid, and then drain the cabbage. Fill jars with the cabbage and put $\frac{1}{4}$ teaspoon cayenne pepper on top of each jar. Cover with cold vinegar and cover tightly.

99

Pickled Gherkins

1·35 kg (3 lb) gherkins
100 g (4 oz) salt
1 litre (2 pints) water
1 litre (2 pints) vinegar
7 g (¼ oz) black peppercorns
7 g (¼ oz) whole allspice
1 teaspoon salt

Wipe the gherkins, put them into a bowl and cover with the 100 g (4 oz) salt dissolved in water. Leave for 3 days, then drain the gherkins. Put the vinegar in a saucepan with the peppercorns, allspice and 1 teaspoon salt. Bring to the boil and simmer for 2 minutes. Pack the gherkins into jars and pour the hot spiced vinegar over them. Cover and leave for 24 hours. Drain off the vinegar, boil it and pour over the gherkins again. Leave for 24 hours and repeat the process. Do this several times until the gherkins are richly green coloured. Cover tightly and store in a dark place.

Pickled Mock Capers (Nasturtium Seeds)

450 g (1 lb) fresh nasturtium seeds
500 ml (1 pint) vinegar
25 g (1 oz) salt
6 peppercorns

Gather the seeds on a dry day when they are young and soft, and wipe them clean. Put them into a dry jar and cover with the vinegar, salt and peppercorns. Cover tightly, and add a few more seeds from day to day if the jar is not full. Leave for a year before eating. These may be used instead of capers.

Pickled Onions

1·8 kg (4 lb) small button onions or shallots
1·5 litres (3 pints) vinegar
3 teaspoons whole allspice
3 teaspoons peppercorns

Peel the onions and pack them into clean dry jars. Put the vinegar into a pan with the allspice and peppercorns and bring to the boil. Remove from heat, leave until completely cold and pour over the onions. Cover tightly and store for 3 months before use.

Marrow Pickle

1 large marrow
cooking salt
1 litre (2 pints) vinegar
½ teaspoon pepper
75 g (3 oz) mustard powder

Peel the marrow and cut it into small cubes. Sprinkle with salt and leave overnight. Drain off the liquid and put the marrow into a saucepan with the vinegar and pepper. Bring to the boil and simmer until the marrow is tender but not broken up. Mix the mustard with a little extra cold vinegar and add to the saucepan. Boil together for 3 minutes, then pack into jars and cover tightly.

Military Pickle

1 marrow
1 cauliflower
450 g (1 lb) runner beans
450 g (1 lb) onions
cooking salt
2 litres (4 pints) vinegar
450 g (1 lb) demerara sugar
7 chillies
25 g (1 oz) turmeric powder
25 g (1 oz) ground ginger
75 g (3 oz) plain flour

Cut up the marrow in small cubes without peeling. Break the cauliflower into small flowerets. Cut the beans into thick chunks. Peel the onions and cut them into chunks unless they are very small and can be used whole. Mix the vegetables together and sprinkle with cooking salt. Leave to stand overnight, and then drain.

Put the vegetables into a large thick saucepan, add the vinegar and boil for 5 minutes. Add the sugar and finely chopped chillies. Mix together the turmeric powder, ginger and flour and beat to a paste with a little extra vinegar. Add to the boiling ingredients and continue to boil for 30 minutes, stirring well to prevent burning. Cool and put into jars, covering tightly with vinegar-proof covers. A cucumber may be added to the vegetables, and 50 g (2 oz) mustard powder and a pinch of nutmeg provide a different flavour.

Runner Bean Pickle

   2·6 kg (6 lb) runner beans
   6 large onions
   100 g (4 oz) plain flour
   1 litre (2 pints) white vinegar
   50 g (2 oz) mustard powder
   450 g (1 lb) sugar
   1 teaspoon ground black pepper
   1 teaspoon turmeric powder

Slice the beans and the onions thinly and cook them in a little water until tender. Drain very thoroughly. Mix the flour with a little of the vinegar, then work in the rest of the vinegar and put in a saucepan with the remaining ingredients and bring to the boil. Stir all the time while boiling until the mixture is thick. Add the beans and onions and continue stirring all the time until the mixture boils again. Put into jars and cover while hot.

Sweet Cucumber Pickle

   1·35 kg (3 lb) cucumbers
   15 g (½ oz) powdered alum
   1 litre (2 pints) water
   900 g (2 lb) sugar
   500 ml (1 pint) vinegar
   50 g (2 oz) whole cloves
   5-cm (2-in) cinnamon stick

Peel the cucumbers thinly and cut them into 7·5-cm (3-in) pieces. Cut each piece into quarters. Cover with the alum dissolved in the water and bring slowly to the boil. Drain and chill the cucumber in iced water. Put the sugar, vinegar, cloves and cinnamon stick into a saucepan, bring to the boil and continue boiling for 5 minutes. Remove the spices. Drain the cucumber and add to the syrup. Simmer for 10 minutes. Leave the cucumber in the syrup overnight.

   Next day, drain off the syrup, boil hard for 1 minute and pour over the cucumbers. Leave overnight and then repeat the process. Do this once more, then remove the cucumber pieces from the syrup and pack them into jars. Boil the syrup and pour over the cucumber pieces. Cool and cover tightly.

Sweet Marrow Pickle

   3·5 kg (8 lb) prepared marrow
   1 litre (2 pints) white vinegar

1·35 kg (3 lb) sugar
5-cm (2-in) cinnamon stick
15 g (½ oz) whole cloves

Prepare the marrow by peeling and scooping out the pith and seeds, and weigh after peeling. Cut the marrow into pieces about 3·5 cm (1½ in) long and 1 cm (½ in) wide. Put the vinegar and sugar into a pan and tie the spices in a piece of muslin and hang it in the vinegar mixture. Bring to the boil. Add the marrow and cook gently, stirring occasionally, until all the pieces of marrow are translucent but keep their shape. Drain and put the marrow in a bowl to cool. Re-boil the vinegar until it becomes syrupy, adding any fluid which runs from the marrow while it is standing. Put the marrow pieces into jars, and when the vinegar syrup has been reduced to 750 ml (1½ pints), take out the spices and pour the boiling liquid on to the marrow. Cover tightly.

Pumpkin Pickle

1 2·2-kg (5-lb) pumpkin
1·5 litres (3 pints) white vinegar
1·35 kg (3 lb) sugar
15 g (½ oz) celery salt
2 pieces ginger root
2 cinnamon sticks
15 g (½ oz) mustard seeds
10 whole cloves

Peel the pumpkin and cut it into small pieces. Boil the vinegar and sugar together, pour it over the pumpkin, and leave overnight. Next day, drain off the liquid and add the spices. Bring to the boil and add the pumpkin pieces. Simmer for 3 hours, put into jars and cover tightly. Keep for 1 month before using.

Sweet Pickled Green Tomatoes

1·2 kg (2½ lb) green tomatoes
225 g (8 oz) onions
cooking salt
225 g (8 oz) sugar
500 ml (1 pint) white vinegar

Slice the tomatoes and onions and sprinkle generously with salt. Leave for 24 hours and drain off the salt liquid completely. Dissolve the sugar in the vinegar and bring to the boil. Add the tomatoes and onions and simmer until tender. Pour into jars and cover tightly while hot.

Beetroot Chutney

900 g (2 lb) beetroot
2 medium-sized onions
450 g (1 lb) apples
225 g (8 oz) sugar
500 ml (1 pint) vinegar
¼ teaspoon ground ginger
½ teaspoon salt
1 tablespoon lemon juice

Boil the beetroot until tender. Cool, peel and cut into small cubes. Peel and cube the onions and apples and put them into a pan with sugar, vinegar, ginger, salt and lemon juice, and boil for 30 minutes. Add the beetroot cubes and simmer for 15 minutes. Cool and bottle and cover tightly.

Blackberry Chutney

2·6 kg (6 lb) blackberries
900 g (2 lb) apples
900 g (2 lb) onions
25 g (1 oz) salt
50 g (2 oz) mustard powder
50 g (2 oz) ground ginger
2 teaspoons ground mace
1 teaspoon cayenne pepper
1 litre (2 pints) vinegar
900 g (2 lb) soft brown sugar

Wash the berries and put them into a thick saucepan. Peel the apples and onions and chop them in small pieces. Put them into the pan with all the other ingredients except the sugar. Cook gently for 1 hour, and then put through a sieve to remove the blackberry pips. Add the brown sugar, stir well and simmer for 45 minutes until thick. Put into jars and cover tightly.

Gooseberry Chutney

1·35 kg (3 lb) green gooseberries
225 g (8 oz) onions
175 g (6 oz) raisins
275 g (10 oz) sugar
500 ml (1 pint) vinegar
15 g (½ oz) ground mixed spice
15 g (½ oz) mustard powder
25 g (1 oz) salt

½ teaspoon cayenne pepper
15 g (½ oz) paprika

Mince the gooseberries and onions together. Mix all the ingredients in a thick pan and simmer for 2 hours until the mixture is a rich brown colour and the consistency of jam. Put into jars and cover tightly.

Marrow and Apple Chutney

1·8 kg (4 lb) prepared marrow
75 g (3 oz) cooking salt
900 g (2 lb) apples
450 g (1 lb) shallots
25 g (1 oz) dried chillies
25 g (1 oz) peppercorns
25 g (1 oz) root ginger
1·5 litres (3 pints) vinegar
450 g (1 lb) sugar

Prepare the marrow by peeling and removing the pith, and weigh after preparation. Cut the marrow into pieces and sprinkle with salt between layers in a bowl. Leave for 12 hours and drain thoroughly.

Chop the peeled apples and shallots and add to the marrow. Tie the chillies, peppercorns and ginger into a piece of muslin and suspend the little bag in the saucepan. Simmer until the marrow is soft, then add the vinegar and sugar. Mix well and simmer to the consistency of jam. Take out the spices, put the chutney into jars and cover tightly.

Marrow and Tomato Chutney

1·8 kg (4 lb) red tomatoes
450 g (1 lb) prepared marrow
225 g (8 oz) onions
15 g (½ oz) salt
pinch cayenne pepper
¼ teaspoon paprika
¼ teaspoon ground cinnamon
¼ teaspoon ground cloves
¼ teaspoon ground allspice
¼ teaspoon ground mace
350 g (12 oz) sugar
250 ml (½ pint) vinegar

Wipe the tomatoes and cut them in pieces. Prepare the marrow by peeling and removing the pith and weigh the flesh after preparation. Peel the onions and cut them in pieces. Put the tomato, marrow and onions through the mincer. Put into a saucepan with the salt and spices and simmer for $1\frac{1}{2}$ hours, stirring occasionally. Add the sugar and vinegar, stir well and continue simmering until brown and thick. Put into jars and cover tightly.

Rhubarb Chutney

900 g (2 lb) rhubarb
225 g (8 oz) onions
675 g (1½ lb) soft brown sugar
225 g (8 oz) sultanas
15 g (½ oz) mustard seeds
1 teaspoon ground mixed spice
1 teaspoon pepper
1 teaspoon ground ginger
1 teaspoon salt
¼ teaspoon cayenne pepper
500 ml (1 pint) vinegar

Wipe the rhubarb and cut it into 2·5-cm (1-in) lengths. Peel the onions and chop them finely. Put all the ingredients into a thick saucepan, and simmer gently, stirring frequently, for about 3 hours until the mixture is a rich brown and the consistency of jam. Put into jars and cover tightly.

Green Tomato Chutney

900 g (2 lb) green tomatoes
900 g (2 lb) apples
100 g (4 oz) shallots
25 g (1 oz) garlic
450 g (1 lb) soft brown sugar
15 g (½ oz) salt
7 g (¼ oz) cayenne pepper
225 g (8 oz) raisins
juice of 2 lemons
500 ml (1 pint) vinegar

Chop the tomatoes finely without peeling. Peel the apples and cut them in small pieces. Peel and chop the shallots and garlic. Mix all the ingredients together and simmer gently for $2\frac{1}{2}$ hours, stirring often, until the chutney is a rich brown and the consistency of jam. Put into jars and cover tightly.

Red Tomato Chutney

450 g (1 lb) red tomatoes

225 g (8 oz) onions
100 g (4 oz) apples
450 g (1 lb) raisins
100 g (4 oz) soft brown sugar
7 g (¼ oz) salt
7 g (¼ oz) ground ginger
pinch cayenne pepper
250 ml (½ pint) vinegar

Skin the tomatoes and peel the onions and apples. Chop the tomatoes, onions and apples and mix with all the other ingredients. Simmer, stirring well, for 2½ hours, until the chutney is a rich brown and the consistency of jam. Put into jars and cover tightly.

Spiced Blackberries

250 ml (½ pint) cider or wine vinegar
7 g (¼ oz) whole allspice
7 g (¼ oz) cardamons
7 g (¼ oz) coriander seed
5-cm (2-in) cinnamon stick
1 bayleaf
450 g (1 lb) sugar
1·2 kg (2½ lb) blackberries
2 rose geranium leaves

Simmer together the vinegar, spices and bayleaf until the vinegar reaches boiling point. Take off the heat and leave to stand for 3 hours. Take out the spices and bayleaf, and dissolve the sugar in the vinegar. Add the blackberries and rose geranium leaves. Bring to the boil and simmer gently for 5 minutes until the blackberries are tender. Lift out the berries with a perforated spoon and put them into warm jars. Boil the vinegar until syrupy, pour over the berries and cover tightly.

Spiced Gooseberries

900 g (2 lb) green gooseberries
225 g (8 oz) soft brown sugar
500 ml (2 pints) white wine vinegar
1 tablespoon mustard powder
2 garlic cloves
350 g (12 oz) raisins
15 g (½ oz) cayenne pepper

Top and tail the gooseberries and cook them with the sugar and half the vinegar until the berries are soft but not broken. Stir in the mustard powder, crushed garlic, raisins and pepper and the remaining cold vinegar. Stir very well and put into jars. Cover tightly and leave for 6 months before using.

Sweetcorn Relish

18 sweetcorn ears
1 small white cabbage
1 head celery
4 medium-sized onions
2 green peppers
2 litres (4 pints) vinegar
450 g (1 lb) sugar
100 g (4 oz) plain flour
50 g (2 oz) salt
½ teaspoon mustard powder
¼ teaspoon cayenne pepper
½ teaspoon turmeric powder

Cut the corn kernels from the cobs with a sharp pointed knife. Finely chop the cabbage, celery, onions and peppers. Put the vegetables into a saucepan with half the vinegar. Mix the remaining ingredients with the rest of the vinegar, and stir into the saucepan. Bring to the boil, then simmer for 45 minutes. Put into jars and cover tightly.

Gooseberry Sauce

1·8 kg (4 lb) green gooseberries
1·35 kg (3 lb) demerara sugar
500 ml (1 pint) white vinegar
4 teaspoons ground cinnamon
3 teaspoons ground allspice
2 teaspoons ground cloves
2 teaspoons cooking salt

Top and tail the gooseberries and put them through a mincer. Put all the ingredients into a thick pan and simmer for 3 hours. Put through a sieve and then reheat. Pour into bottles and cover tightly.

Tomato Sauce

1·8 kg (4 lb) red tomatoes
4 large onions
450 g (1 lb) demerara sugar

25 g (1 oz) salt
50 g (2 oz) peppercorns
15 g (½ oz) whole cloves
2 teaspoons cayenne pepper
500 ml (1 pint) vinegar

Slice the tomatoes and onions and put all the ingredients into a thick pan. Simmer gently for 2 hours, stirring occasionally. Rub through a fine sieve, leaving nothing but the spices, seeds and skin in the sieve. Bring the pulp to the boil and boil for 5 minutes. Cool completely and bottle.

Jams, Jellies and Sweet Preserves

Delicious jams, jellies and other sweet preserves may be made from quite small quantities of fruit, and it is useful to make a variety of preserves from surplus produce. The family will appreciate a small quantity of a number of different varieties far more than huge amounts of any single recipe.

Sweet preserves may be made from single fruits or from a mixture of two or more; though the fruit may be surplus, it must still be fresh and sound, rather than mushy or over-ripe. The setting quality of jam depends on its pectin content, which is particularly high in apples, blackcurrants and redcurrants, gooseberries, damsons and plums, so that the addition of these fruits or their extracted juices will help the setting of such fruit as strawberries which are low in pectin content. A similar result may be achieved with acid in the form of lemon juice or citric acid powder (obtainable from the chemist). To 1·8 kg (4 lb) low-pectin fruit or vegetables such as marrow, allow 2 tablespoons lemon juice or ½ teaspoon citric acid powder, or 125 ml (¼ pint) extracted redcurrant or gooseberry juice. The other important ingredient of jam is sugar; special preserving sugar dissolves quickly, but is more expensive than other types of sugar. Brown sugar and honey affect the colour, flavour and setting quality of the jam.

A large saucepan is necessary for making jam, and this should not be made of zinc or iron. Unchipped enamel is suitable, or aluminium. Copper will keep green fruit such as gooseberries green, but will spoil the colour of red fruit. The pan should be wide enough to allow rapid evaporation of liquid which will speed up setting, and the pan should be thick to withstand burning. A long-handled wooden spoon should be used for stirring. If jellies are to be made frequently, it is worth buying a jelly bag which can be supported by a stand, or suspended between the legs of a chair turned upside-down. If this is not available, use an old well-boiled tea towel tied with string, suspended between chair legs.

Before preparing jam or jelly, get the jars ready. Use jam jars, honey jars, instant coffee jars or preserving jars. These can be used with existing screwtop lids, with special plastic covers, or with transparent paper covers. Sets of waxed paper discs, transparent covers and labels in packets are worth buying as they give the jam a neat appearance as well as making it clean and airproof. Jars should be freshly washed before use and kept warm in a low oven so that they are dry and sterile before filling.

JAM-MAKING

Sort the fruit and discard any damaged pieces, leaves and stems. When ready to cook the jam, wash the fruit gently and peel or stone if necessary. Weigh ingredients carefully, as there must be a correct balance between fruit and sugar. The fruit must be cooked slowly to extract pectin, soften skins and retain a good colour. Sugar has to be stirred in carefully to dissolve before further cooking, and the sugar may first be warmed slightly in the oven so that it dissolves more quickly. Jam then has to be boiled rapidly to setting point, which can be tested by dropping a little jam on a cold saucer, leaving it until cold, and then pushing it with your finger. If the jam forms a skin and wrinkles when pushed, it is ready, and the pan should be taken off the heat at once. Over-boiled jam will not set and will have an unattractive colour and texture.

Skim the jam, then pour it into clean, dry warm jars. Whole fruit jam should be left to stand in the pan for 10 minutes after it has been taken from the heat, before it is stirred and potted; this will prevent fruit rising to the top. Fill the jars completely to the top and cover at once with waxed discs. Moisten transparent covers on one side only, then fit over the jars and secure with elastic bands. Label carefully with the variety and date of making, then wipe the jars and store them in a cool, dark, dry place.

A few sweet preserves are made by layering fruit or vegetables with sugar and leaving overnight before cooking. This results in a syrupy preserve which is more suitable for some ingredients such as marrow.

Jelly is made by preparing the fruit as for jam and cooking it until tender. The fruit and liquid are then tipped into a jelly bag or clean cloth and left to drip slowly into a bowl. Do not squeeze the bag, as this will make the jelly cloudy. The juice then has to be measured so that the correct proportion of sugar can be added, dissolved, and then boiled in the juice. Jelly is tested in the same way as jam, and when it reaches setting point, it should be poured quickly into small jars. Small jars are best, as jelly looks less attractive if it is disturbed too often by a spoon when serving. If jelly is left to cool before being poured into jars, bubbles will form and it will look unattractive. Store in jars following the instructions for jam (previous page).

Blackberry Jam

2·6 kg (6 lb) blackberries
125 ml ($\frac{1}{4}$ pint) water
4 teaspoons lemon juice
2·6 kg (6 lb) sugar

Put the blackberries into a pan with the water and lemon juice. Simmer until the fruit is very soft. Stir in the sugar until dissolved, then boil hard to setting point. Pour into hot jars and cover.

Blackberry and Marrow Jam

900 g (2 lb) blackberries
1·8 kg (4 lb) prepared marrow
grated rind of 1 lemon
juice of 2 lemons
500 ml (1 pint) water
1·5 kg (3$\frac{1}{2}$ lb) sugar

Put the blackberries and the marrow flesh cut into cubes into a pan with the lemon rind and juice and the water. Simmer until soft, and then put through a sieve. Stir in the sugar until dissolved, then boil hard to setting point. Pour into hot jars and cover.

Blackberry and Rhubarb Jam

1·8 kg (4 lb) blackberries
375 ml ($\frac{3}{4}$ pint) water
900 g (2 lb) rhubarb
sugar

Simmer the blackberries in water until tender and put through a sieve. Cut up the rhubarb and add it to the blackberry pulp. Simmer until soft. Weigh the fruit and add 450 g (1 lb) sugar to each 450 g (1 lb) pulp. Stir in sugar until dissolved, then boil hard to setting point. Pour into hot jars and cover.

Blackcurrant Jam

1·8 kg (4 lb) blackcurrants
1·5 litres (3 pints) water
2·6 kg (6 lb) sugar

Remove the stems from the currants and wash the fruit. Put the fruit into a pan with the water and simmer gently until the fruit is very tender. Stir often to prevent burning. Stir in the sugar until dissolved and then boil hard to setting point. Pour into hot jars and cover.

Four Fruit Jam

225 g (8 oz) blackcurrants
3 tablespoons water
225 g (8 oz) redcurrants
225 g (8 oz) raspberries
225 g (8 oz) strawberries
900 g (2 lb) sugar

Put the blackcurrants in a pan with water and simmer until tender. Add the other fruit and simmer for 10 minutes. Stir in the sugar until dissolved, then boil hard to setting point. Pour into hot jars and cover.

Green Gooseberry Jam

1·8 kg (4 lb) green gooseberries
500 ml (1 pint) water
1·8 kg (4 lb) sugar
1 lemon

Top and tail the gooseberries and simmer with the water until soft. Stir in the sugar until dissolved, and add the grated rind and juice of the lemon. Boil hard for exactly 10 minutes, then pour into hot jars and cover.

Marrow Ginger

2·6 kg (6 lb) prepared marrow
4 lemons
75 g (3 oz) root ginger
2·6 kg (6 lb) sugar

Prepare the marrow by peeling and removing the seeds and pith, then weighing the flesh. Cut the marrow into cubes and steam until just tender. Put into a bowl with the grated rind and juice of the lemons, and the bruised root ginger. Stir in the sugar and leave to stand for 24 hours. Put into a thick pan and heat carefully until the sugar is dissolved. Cook gently until the marrow is transparent, and the syrup is thick and will set when put onto a cold plate. Remove the pieces of ginger, and put the marrow and syrup into warm jars, covering at once.

Melon and Raspberry Jam

1·5 kg (3¼ lb) prepared melon
1·8 kg (4 lb) sugar
1 lemon
450 g (1 lb) raspberries

Use a melon which is not too ripe. Peel the melon, cut it into cubes and put it into a bowl in layers with the sugar and the juice of the lemon. Leave for 12 hours. Bring to the boil and add the raspberries. Cook gently for 30 minutes. Pour into hot jars and cover.

Pumpkin Preserve

1 medium-sized pumpkin
1·8 kg (4 lb) sugar
225 g (8 oz) butter
6 lemons

Peel the pumpkin and remove the seeds. Cut it into pieces and steam for 30 minutes. Drain in a muslin bag for 24 hours. Weigh the remaining pulp (1·8 kg (4 lb) is needed for the remaining ingredients). Put into a pan with the sugar, butter and the grated rind and juice of the lemons. Bring to the boil slowly, and then boil gently for 20 minutes. Pour into hot jars and cover. Because of the fat content, do not try to keep this preserve more than 2 months.

Raspberry Preserve

25 g (1 oz) butter
1·35 kg (3 lb) raspberries
1·35 kg (3 lb) sugar

Warm a pan and rub it with the butter. Put in the raspberries and heat very slowly until the juice runs. Warm the sugar in the oven. Add the warm sugar to the raspberries and beat over a low heat for 30 minutes. Pour into hot jars and cover. This jam has the colour and flavour of fresh fruit.

Rhubarb and Orange Preserve

1·8 kg (4 lb) rhubarb
6 oranges
1·8 kg (4 lb) sugar
½ teaspoon citric acid

Cut the rhubarb into short pieces. Grate the rind from the oranges and squeeze out the juice. Put the rhubarb, orange rind and juice into a bowl and leave for 12 hours. Put into a pan with the sugar and add the acid. Bring to the boil, stirring well until the sugar has dissolved. Boil hard to setting point, pour into hot jars and cover.

Strawberry Jam

1·8 kg (4 lb) strawberries
1 teaspoon citric acid powder
1·5 kg (3½ lb) sugar

Put the strawberries in a pan with the acid and simmer for 30 minutes until the fruit is soft. Stir in the sugar until dissolved, then boil hard to setting point. Cool for 15 minutes, stir well, pour into hot jars and cover.

Green Tomato Conserve

1·35 kg (3 lb) sugar
500 ml (1 pint) water
1·8 kg (4 lb) green tomatoes
1 orange
1 lemon

Put 450 g (1 lb) sugar with the water in a saucepan and simmer until the liquid is syrupy, but not coloured. Use small green tomatoes which are just turning yellow, and poach them in the syrup very gently for 15 minutes. Leave for 24 hours. Do this every day for 7 days. Remove the tomatoes carefully and cut them in half. Pack into jars. Add the remaining sugar to the syrup with the grated peel of the orange and lemon. Cook until the syrup is clear and thick, pour over the fruit and cover tightly. This conserve is best eaten with thick cream.

Green Tomato Jam

1 orange
900 g (2 lb) green tomatoes
675 g (1½ lb) sugar

Cut the peel from the orange very thinly, removing all the white pith.

Shred the rind and cook in a little water until tender, then drain. Cut the tomatoes in very small pieces, taking out the pips, and mix the flesh with the cooked orange rind. Simmer together for 45 minutes, and then stir in the sugar until dissolved. Bring to the boil and boil fast to setting point, which will take about 20 minutes. Put into warm jars and cover.

Red Tomato Conserve

2·2 kg (5 lb) red tomatoes
1·8 kg (4 lb) sugar
175 g (6 oz) raisins
1 orange
1 lemon
100 g (4 oz) walnut kernels

Cover the tomatoes with boiling water, drain, and take off the skins. Cut up the tomatoes in small pieces, removing the pips. Put into a thick pan with the sugar, and cook gently for $1\frac{1}{2}$ hours. Add the raisins and the orange and lemon peeled and cut into very small pieces. Simmer for 30 minutes. Stir in chopped walnuts and continue cooking for 10 minutes. Put into warm jars and cover.

Tomato and Melon Jam

1·35 kg (3 lb) red tomatoes
900 g (2 lb) prepared melon
2 lemons
40 g (1¼ oz) preserved ginger
1·8 kg (4 lb) sugar

Skin the tomatoes and cut them in slices, removing the pips. Peel the melon, remove the seeds, and weigh the flesh. Cut the melon into cubes. Put the tomatoes into a thick pan with the melon. Do not peel the lemons, but cut them in thin slices, removing the pips. Add to the pan, together with finely chopped ginger. Simmer until the mixture is soft, and then stir in the sugar until dissolved. Bring to the boil, simmer until thick, put into warm jars and cover.

Black Butter

redcurrants
blackcurrants
gooseberries
strawberries
sugar

A mixture of some or all of the fruits can be used. For each 900 g (2 lb) fruit, allow 450 g (1 lb) sugar. Prepare and mix the fruits and heat them gently in a pan until the juices start to run. Stir in the sugar until dissolved, and boil until very thick. Pour into small hot jars and cover.

Blackberry Cheese

1·8 kg (4 lb) blackberries
2 teaspoons citric acid
sugar

Wash the blackberries and put them into a pan with just enough water to cover, and the acid. Bring to the boil, and simmer gently until the fruit is soft. Put through a sieve and weigh the pulp. Allow 450 g (1 lb) sugar to each 450 g (1 lb) of pulp. Stir in the sugar until dissolved, then boil and stir until the mixture is thick. Pour into hot jars and cover.

Gooseberry Cheese

1·35 kg (3 lb) green gooseberries
250 ml (¼ pint) water
sugar

Top and tail the gooseberries and simmer in the water until soft. Put them through a sieve and weigh the pulp. Allow 350 g (12 oz) sugar to each 450 g (1 lb) pulp. Stir the sugar until dissolved and bring to the boil. Cook gently, stirring all the time, until the mixture is thick. Pour into hot jars and cover.

Tomato Honey

450 g (1 lb) red tomatoes
1 lemon
450 g (1 lb) sugar

Chop the tomatoes and put them into a thick pan with the grated rind of the lemon. Simmer until soft, and put the mixture through a sieve. Put into the pan with the sugar and juice of the lemon, and stir until the sugar has dissolved. Boil rapidly until thick, put into hot jars and cover. This makes an unusual filling for tarts.

Alpine Strawberries in Syrup

900 g (2 lb) Alpine strawberries
350 g (12 oz) sugar

Put the strawberries into a bowl and sprinkle with sugar. Leave to stand overnight. Drain off the syrup the next day, bring to the boil, and boil for 3 minutes. Add the strawberries and simmer 30 minutes. Pour into small hot jars and cover. The strawberries will be floating in syrup, and are delicious with ice cream.

Blackberry Jelly

> *1·8 kg (4 lb) blackberries*
> *juice of 2 lemons*
> *250 ml (½ pint) water*
> *sugar*

Use slightly under-ripe blackberries for this recipe. Put them into a pan with the lemon juice and water and simmer for 1 hour until the fruit is soft. Strain through a jelly bag and measure the juice. Allow 450 g (1 lb) sugar to each 500 ml (1 pint) of juice. Heat the juice gently, stirring in the sugar until dissolved. Boil hard to setting point and pour into hot jars.

Blackcurrant and Redcurrant Jelly

> *450 g (1 lb) blackcurrants*
> *450 g (1 lb) redcurrants*
> *500 ml (1 pint) water*
> *sugar*

Simmer the currants in the water until soft. Strain through a jelly bag and measure the juice. Allow 450 g (1 lb) sugar to each 500 ml (1 pint) of juice. Heat the juice gently, stirring in the sugar until dissolved. Boil hard to setting point and pour into hot jars.

Raspberry and Redcurrant Jelly

> *900 g (2 lb) raspberries*
> *900 g (2 lb) redcurrants*
> *500 ml (1 pint) water*
> *sugar*

Put the fruit into the water and simmer gently until the fruit is very soft. Strain through a jelly bag and measure the juice. Allow 450 g (1 lb) sugar to each 500 ml (1 pint) of juice. Heat the juice gently, stirring in the sugar until dissolved. Boil hard to setting point, and pour into small hot jars. This makes an excellent glaze for cakes and flans.

Redcurrant Jelly with Wild Strawberries

> *1·35 kg (3 lb) redcurrants*
> *250 ml (½ pint) water*

sugar
225 g (8 oz) wild strawberries

Heat the currants with the water and simmer until the fruit is pulped. Strain through a jelly bag. Measure the juice and allow 450 g (1 lb) sugar to each 500 ml (1 pint) of juice. Stir until the sugar has dissolved and boil rapidly to setting point. About 5 minutes before jelly is ready, add the strawberries. Pour into small jars and cover.

Spiced Redcurrant Jelly

1·35 kg (3 lb) redcurrants
500 ml (1 pint) water
125 ml (¼ pint) white vinegar
3 cloves
5-cm (2-in) stick cinnamon
sugar

Simmer the redcurrants in the vinegar with the spices. When the fruit is completely soft, strain through a jelly bag or several thicknesses of muslin. Measure the liquid and allow 450 g (1 lb) sugar to each 500 ml (1 pint) of liquid. Stir the sugar into the liquid until it dissolves, then boil hard until a little sets on a cold plate. Pour into small jars and cover.

Strawberry Jelly

900 g (2 lb) strawberries
juice of 1 lemon
sugar

Heat the strawberries very gently with the lemon juice until the fruit is soft. Strain through a jelly bag and measure the juice. Allow 450 g (1 lb) sugar to each 500 ml (1 pint) of juice. Heat the juice gently, stirring in the sugar until dissolved. Boil hard to setting point and pour into hot jars.

Strawberry and Redcurrant Jelly

450 g (1 lb) strawberries
225 g (8 oz) redcurrants
4 tablespoons water
sugar

Put the strawberries and redcurrants into a pan with the water. Simmer until soft. Strain through a jelly bag and measure the juice. Allow 450 g (1 lb) sugar to each 500 ml (1 pint) of juice. Heat the juice gently, stirring in the sugar until dissolved. Boil hard to setting point and pour into hot jars.

Tomato Jelly

1·35 kg (3 lb) red tomatoes
3 tablespoons lemon juice
5-cm (2-in) stick cinnamon
675 g (1½ lb) sugar

Cut the tomatoes into pieces and simmer them very gently until soft. Strain through a jelly bag. Heat the juice with the lemon juice and cinnamon stick and stir in sugar until dissolved. Boil hard to setting point. Remove the cinnamon stick and pour into small hot jars.

Wines, Cordials, Liqueurs and Soft Drinks

Drinks made from garden vegetables, fruit, herbs and honey are delicious, nourishing and money-saving. It is easy to use honey instead of sugar to sweeten drinks, and simple drinks can be made by blending soft fruit and yoghurt, or by liquidising raw vegetables (an electric blender is invaluable for this purpose). More ambitiously, wines and liqueurs may be made for the store-cupboard.

Wine-making is not difficult, and does not require an enormous range of equipment. Country people managed for centuries with everyday kitchen containers and there is no need for investment in anything elaborate until you have tried one or two wines and decided you might want to go in for more intensive production. Try a few of the wines in this chapter, and then invest in a book which will tell you about a huge variety of drinks you can make. Basically, you need a container, which can be a big earthenware or ovenglass bowl, and a wooden spoon or masher for crushing the raw materials. Either buy a fermentation jar, or use one which has contained cider (these come in 2-litre ($\frac{1}{2}$-gallon) and 4-litre (1-gallon) sizes). A fermentation lock costs a few pence and is available in the wine-making department of a chemist; clean bottles and corks can also be bought there. Modern thinking decrees the use of wine yeasts rather than baker's or dried yeast, as wine yeasts give a better flavour and fermentation. A general-purpose yeast may be used, or one which is suited to the character of the finished product—for example, fruits such as blackberries are good fermented with port yeast, while the lighter gooseberry is better with a champagne or tokay yeast. Sometimes a yeast nutrient is recommended, or grape tannin, and also Campden tablets for sterilisation. All these can easily be bought at the chemist and should be used as recommended on the packets. Don't be tempted to try your home-made wine too soon. Nearly all wines are better for at least 6 months' storage, but a year gives even nicer results. Start with ingredients you feel will give you a fairly familiar flavour, such as raspberries or blackcurrants and then progress to herb and vegetable wines. It is even possible to make wine from such unlikely ingredients as broad beans and peapods.

Old-fashioned cordials and liqueurs are very easy indeed to make and delicious to drink. While it may seem expensive to buy brandy for this purpose, the drinks are concentrated in flavour and very little is needed for an after-dinner drink. When fruit is added to brandy, liquid is drawn off and the result is that 1 bottle of brandy will usually make about $1\frac{1}{2}$ bottles of liqueur, which brings the price down well below a similar drink from a shop.

Honey Mint Syrup

225 g (8 oz) honey
250 ml ($\frac{1}{2}$ pint) water
125 ml ($\frac{1}{4}$ pint) lemon juice
6 tablespoons fresh mint leaves

Put the honey, water and lemon juice into a saucepan and add the finely-chopped mint. Bring to the boil and boil for 10 minutes. Strain and cool and store in the refrigerator. Dilute to taste with iced water.

Honey Lemonade

juice of 1 lemon
3 tablespoons honey
250 ml ($\frac{1}{2}$ pint) water

Stir the lemon juice into the honey until the honey has melted. Add the water and pour over ice cubes in individual glasses. Garnish with a sprig of borage or mint.

Honey Tea

225 g (8 oz) dried prunes
225 g (8 oz) honey
juice of 4 lemons

juice of 4 oranges
250 ml (½ pint) strong tea

Soak the prunes overnight in enough water to cover them. Stir in the honey and bring slowly to the boil. Simmer until the prunes are tender but not broken. Strain off the liquid (the prunes may be eaten separately) and mix with the lemon juice, orange juice and cold tea. Mix well and chill before serving.

Honey Refresher

125 ml (¼ pint) natural yoghurt
juice of 1 orange
2 teaspoons honey

Whisk together the yoghurt, orange juice and honey until well mixed. These amounts make enough for 1 person.

Herb Beer

large bunch mixed herbs
25 g (1 oz) hops
8 litres (2 gallons) water
900 g (2 lb) sugar
15 g (½ oz) yeast

Use parsley, thyme, sage and mint for the herbs. Put the herbs and hops into the water and boil for 1 hour. Strain on to the sugar and stir until dissolved. Cool and add the yeast. Leave to stand for 12 hours, then put into bottles. Hops are obtainable from health food stores and chemists.

Blackcurrant Wine

1·35 kg (3 lb) blackcurrants
4 litres (1 gallon) water
1·35 kg (3 lb) sugar
juice of 1 lemon
125 ml (¼ pint) cold tea
wine yeast
yeast nutrient

Put the fruit into a container and pour over enough water (from the 4 litres (1 gallon)) to cover the currants. Mash well and leave to stand for 48 hours, stirring often. Strain off the liquid. Make a syrup by stirring the sugar into the remaining hot water and add to the blackcurrant liquid with the lemon juice and cold tea. Cool and pour into a fermentation jar with the wine yeast and nutrient. Ferment until the bubbles cease to rise and syphon off into bottles. Store for 6 months before drinking. For a heavy port-type wine, add 100 g (4 oz) raisins, use port wine yeast, and omit the yeast nutrient.

Carrot Wine

2·6 kg (6 lb) carrots
4 litres (1 gallon) water
1·8 kg (4 lb) sugar
450 g (1 lb) wheat
1 lemon
1 orange
wine yeast
100 g (4 oz) raisins

Scrub and peel the carrots and boil until tender in water. Strain the liquid over the sugar, wheat and fruit rinds and stir well. When lukewarm, add fruit juices, yeast and raisins. Stir well and leave for 7 days, stirring daily. Remove rinds, but not raisins, and pour into fermentation jar with lock. Bottle when all fermentation has ceased. Wheat is obtainable from health food shops.

Celery Wine

1·8 kg (4 lb) celery stalks and leaves
2 lemons
1 orange
25 g (1 oz) root ginger
4 litres (1 gallon) water
1·5 kg (3½ lb) sugar
wine yeast
yeast nutrient

Cut the celery into small pieces and add to the thinly peeled rinds of the lemons and orange. Add the crushed ginger and the water, and bring to the boil, simmering until the celery is soft. Strain on to the sugar and stir well until the sugar has dissolved. Add the lemon and orange juice. Strain into a fermentation jar, add the yeast and nutrient. Ferment until the bubbles cease rising and syphon off into bottles. Store for 6 months before using.

Gooseberry Wine

2·2 kg (5 lb) gooseberries
4 litres (1 gallon) water
juice of 1 lemon

125 ml (¼ pint) cold tea
1 teaspoon pectic enzyme
1·2 kg (2½ lb) sugar
champagne yeast

Cut up the fruit, put it into a container and pour over enough boiling water to cover (from the 4 litres (1 gallon)). Crush and mash periodically for 2 days. Strain off the gooseberry juice and add the lemon juice, tea and pectic enzyme. Make a syrup with the sugar and remaining water and add this to the juice. Cool, add the yeast and put into a fermentation jar. Ferment until bubbles cease to rise and then syphon off into bottles. Store for 6 months before using.

Parsley Wine

450 g (1 lb) fresh parsley
piece of root ginger
2 oranges
2 lemons
4 litres (1 gallon) water
1·8 kg (4 lb) sugar
1 teaspon grape tannin
wine yeast
yeast nutrient

Boil the parsley, bruised ginger, orange and lemon rinds in the water for 20 minutes. Strain on to the sugar and stir well. When the liquid is lukewarm, stir in the juice of the oranges and lemons, together with the grape tannin, yeast and nutrient. Stir, cover, and leave for 24 hours. Pour into a fermentation jar and ferment until bubbles cease to rise. Syphon off into bottles and leave for 6 months before using.

Parsnip Wine

1·8 kg (4 lb) parsnips
4 litres (1 gallon) water
1 teaspoon ground ginger
2 lemons
1 orange
1·35 kg (3 lb) sugar
wine yeast

Scrub the parsnips, but do not peel them. Cut into 0·5–1-cm (¼–½-in) slices. Boil the parsnips in the water with ground ginger and fruit rinds until tender. Place the sugar in a container and strain over the parsnip liquid. Stir and leave to cool. When the liquid has cooled to lukewarm, add the fruit juices and yeast. Cover closely and leave for 24 hours. Pour into a jar, insert an airlock and leave to ferment. When all fermentation has ceased, syphon into bottles.

Potato Wine

2·2 kg (5 lb) potatoes
4 litres (1 gallon) water
2 lemons
1 orange
1 teaspoon ground ginger
1·5 kg (3½ lb) demerara sugar
wine yeast
100 g (4 oz) seedless raisins

Scrub the potatoes and cut them into large pieces. Boil in the water for 15 minutes and strain off the liquid while the potatoes are still quite firm. Boil the liquid again with the fruit rinds and ginger for 10 minutes, adding more water if the level has dropped below 4 litres (1 gallon). Place the sugar in a container and pour over the boiling liquid. Stir well, and when lukewarm, add fruit juices and yeast. Cover and leave to ferment, stirring daily. When fermentation slows, pour into a fermentation jar, add raisins and insert an airlock. Leave for at least 9 months, then syphon into bottles.

Raspberry Wine

1·35 kg (3 lb) raspberries
4 litres (1 gallon) water
1 Campden tablet
1·35 kg (3 lb) sugar
juice of 1 lemon
wine yeast
yeast nutrient

Put the raspberries into a bowl and pour on boiling water. Add the Campden tablet and leave covered for 2 days, stirring often. Strain and squeeze the liquid on to the sugar, stirring well until the sugar has dissolved. Add the lemon juice, yeast and nutrient and put into a fermentation jar. Leave until bubbles cease to rise and then syphon off into bottles. Leave for 6 months before using.

Rose Petal Wine

350 g (12 oz) scented rose petals

4 litres (1 gallon) water
1·35 kg (3 lb) sugar
wine yeast
large stoned raisins (one for each bottle)

Put the rose petals into a bowl and add 1 litre (2 pints) boiling water. Crush the petals well with a wooden spoon. Strain into a fermentation jar. Boil 1 litre (2 pints) water and pour over the petals, crushing and straining again. Dissolve the sugar in the remaining water and add to the jar with the yeast. Fit a fermentation lock and leave in a cool place for 14 days. Syphon into bottles, add raisins and insert corks. Keep for 6 months before using.

Mead

1·8 kg (4 lb) honey
4 litres (1 gallon) water
juice of 1 lemon
all-purpose wine yeast
yeast nutrient

Use a wine yeast (available from the wine-making department of the chemist) for this honey wine and a commercial yeast nutrient which will ensure a good fermentation. Stir the honey into the water and bring to the boil. Leave to cool, and then stir in the lemon juice, yeast and nutrient. Put into a fermentation jar and fit with an airlock. Leave to ferment, which will take much longer than it does for fruit and flower wines, until no more bubbles are passing. When the wine is clear, and there is sludge on the bottom of the jar, syphon off the wine into bottles and cork. Mead is best stored for a year before using, but can be used after three months.

Melomel

This is the name for a fruit-flavoured mead which is made by using fruit juice instead of water. It can also be made with rosehips: prepare in the same way, but boil 1·8 kg (4 lb) rosehips in the water for 10 minutes, cool and mash, and strain through muslin. Make the liquid up to 4 litres (1 gallon) and continue as for mead. Sherry yeast may be used for this wine.

Metheglin

This is a spiced mead, flavoured in a variety of ways. Add 25 g (1 oz) hops and 15 g ($\frac{1}{2}$ oz) crushed root ginger to the liquid *or* add 2 cloves and 7 g ($\frac{1}{4}$ oz) cinnamon stick. Alternative flavourings are very small quantities of marjoram, lemon balm, mace, lemon or orange peel, rosemary, coriander, caraway or aniseed.

Cyser

This is mead made with pure apple juice instead of water. Halve the quantity of honey, and omit the lemon juice and yeast nutrient as these are unnecessary with fruit juice.

Pyment

Prepare as for cyser, but substitute grape juice for apple juice.

Hippocras

Flavour grape-juice Pyment with the herbs and spices used for Metheglin.

Sack

4 fennel roots (Florence fennel)
2 sprays rue
8 litres (2 gallons) water
1·8 kg (4 lb) honey
wine yeast
yeast nutrient

Wash the fennel roots and rue leaves and simmer in half the water for 1 hour. Strain the liquid on to the honey. Put into a saucepan with the remaining water and simmer for 2 hours, skimming occasionally. Take off the heat and cool to lukewarm. Add the yeast and nutrient and put into a fermentation jar, leaving it to stand in a warm place. Ferment until bubbles cease to rise, and then syphon off into bottles. Store for 6 months before using.

Angelica Liqueur

450 g (1 lb) angelica stalks
500 ml (1 pint) brandy
7-g ($\frac{1}{4}$-oz) stick cinnamon
1 clove
blade mace
225 g (8 oz) sugar

Cut the angelica stalks into small pieces and put them into a preserving jar with the brandy. Add the spices, cover the jar and leave for 4 weeks in a sunny place. Dissolve the sugar in a little water and stir it into the brandy. Strain through a muslin-lined sieve and bottle. Drink as a liqueur, or use as a flavouring, particularly for rhubarb dishes. Angelica stalks are at their best in April. Later they become too tough and 'woody' to use.

Blackberry Cordial

900 g (2 lb) ripe blackberries
500 ml (1 pint) white vinegar
450 g (1 lb) sugar
225 g (8 oz) honey

Put the blackberries into a bowl and pour on the vinegar. Leave to stand for 7 days, stirring well and pressing the blackberries frequently to extract the juices. Strain the liquid into a saucepan and add the sugar and honey. Boil for 5 minutes, cool completely and pour into dark bottles so the cordial does not lose its colour. Cork and store in a cool place. Dilute with hot or cold water to drink.

Blackberry Liqueur

675 g (1½ lb) blackberries
2 cloves
15-g (½-oz) stick cinnamon
500 ml (1 pint) brandy
675 g (1½ lb) sugar

Clean the fruit and mash it well. Add the spices and pour on the brandy. Leave for 3 days, and strain off the liquid. Dissolve the sugar in a little water, cool and stir into the blackberry liquid. Stir well and bottle. Drink as a liqueur or use as a flavouring.

Marrow Rum

1 large firm ripe marrow
demerara sugar

Use a very firm marrow which is too tough for cooking, or for cutting with a knife. Saw through the stalk end and scoop out the seeds and pulp. Fill the marrow cavity completely with sugar. Put the top back on and tape securely in place. Put the marrow into a bag made of strong cloth and hang it in a cool dry place. After 2 weeks, fill the marrow with sugar again, seal the top, and hang in the bag. After 4 weeks, the marrow will begin to drip. Take the marrow from the bag and make a hole where the sugar is beginning to drip. Put a funnel into a bottle and cover it with muslin. Let the liquid run through this covered funnel. Cork the bottles lightly as fermentation will soon begin. In a few weeks, when fermentation has ceased, cork firmly. Keep for a year before using.

Raspberry Brandy

450 g (1 lb) raspberries
1 bottle brandy
225 g (8 oz) sugar

Put the raspberries into a jar with the brandy and leave to stand for 2 months. Add the sugar and stir well until dissolved. Mix well and strain off the liquid into bottles. The raspberries may be eaten as a delicious pudding. This makes a beautiful red liqueur, and using fruit in this way produces 1½ bottles of liqueur for 1 bottle brandy.

Rose Cordial

900 g (2 lb) scented rose petals
1 litre (2 pints) water
225 g (8 oz) sugar
250 ml (¼ pint) brandy
25-g (1-oz) stick cinnamon
25 g (1 oz) coriander seeds

Put half the rose petals into a basin and pour over the hot water. Cover and leave to infuse for 24 hours. Strain off the liquid and pour it over the remaining petals. Leave this mixture for 48 hours, and then strain again. Stir in the sugar, brandy and spices and put into a jar. Cover and leave for 2 weeks. Strain through muslin and put into bottles. Serve as a liqueur.

Sunflower Cordial

50 g (2 oz) sunflower seeds
1 piece root ginger
1 litre (2 pints) water
50 g (2 oz) honey
2 tablespoons brandy

Put the sunflower seeds into a pan with the crushed root ginger and water and simmer for 1 hour. Add the honey, strain and add the brandy. Drink hot or chilled as a refreshing tonic.

Lotions, Potions and Natural Remedies

The traditional uses of herbs and honey for health and beauty are based on the well-tried qualities of these ingredients. Countrywomen handed down their knowledge of the ways in which various plants soothed or stimulated both externally and internally, and these homely recipes are just as effective today.

MEDICINAL HERBS

Many herbs can be grown specifically for their medicinal qualities. They do not produce immediate effects, but gradually restore health and vigour. They are supplementary to qualified medical advice and do not replace it. Both medicinal and culinary herbs have very individual properties which help to *avoid* minor medical problems. An obvious example is sage, which reduces the effect of greasy foods and promotes good digestion, therefore preventing flatulence when eaten in traditional manner with such fat meats as pork, duck or goose.

In general, it is the fresh green or dried leaf that contains the important properties. Gather the leaves of the chosen plant, put them in a teapot or other covered container and pour on boiling water. Leave the mixture to stand for a few minutes, after which it is ready to drink.

So that you can have ample winter supplies of the plants, it is a good idea to dry them. Towards the end of the summer, on a dry warm day, gather the leaves or roots needed and spread them out in a sunny position away from moisture. Turn them every few days until quite dry, and discard any dirty or mouldy leaf. Store in a cool dry place in sacks or, for smaller quantities, in jars.

Angelica

Leaves, stems, seeds and roots can all be used and make an excellent tonic. Infuse a handful of leaves, stems, seeds, or 25 g (1 oz) root in 250 ml ($\frac{1}{2}$ pint) boiling water. Drink hot once or twice a day, taking up to 250 ml ($\frac{1}{2}$ pint) a day.

Borage

Use leaves and stems, and infuse 25 g (1 oz) leaves in 125 ml ($\frac{1}{4}$ pint) boiling water for 15 minutes. Take 125 ml ($\frac{1}{4}$ pint) four times a day, or 250 ml ($\frac{1}{2}$ pint) before sleeping at night.

Calendula

Infuse 25 g (1 oz) leaves or flower buds in 250 ml ($\frac{1}{2}$ pint) boiling water. Drink 125 ml ($\frac{1}{4}$ pint) twice a day, or 250 ml ($\frac{1}{2}$ pint) before sleeping at night. Good for skin troubles and warts, recommended for strengthening a weak heart, eliminating varicose veins, ulcers, sickness, diarrhoea and toothache.

Camomile

Infuse 15 g ($\frac{1}{2}$ oz) flowers in 500 ml (1 pint) boiling water, and take three times a day in wineglassfuls. As a tonic, take up to 250 ml ($\frac{1}{2}$ pint) a day. This is a good remedy for insomnia, and also relieves pain, soothes stomachs and painful periods.

Catnip

Use leaves or flower buds and infuse 25 g (1 oz) leaves in 500 ml (1 pint) boiling water. Take 125 ml ($\frac{1}{4}$ pint) a day as needed. This has a gentle action on the digestive system, relieving wind and hiccups. It is recommended for difficult periods and as a painkiller.

Cayenne

Use ripe dry fruit and grind to a powder. Add a pinch of cayenne to 250 ml ($\frac{1}{2}$ pint) boiling water, and take 1 dessertspoon twice a day. A good purifier, reputedly warding off infectious diseases and colds.

Comfrey

A plant high in vitamins and minerals, containing in particular Vitamin B_{12}. Use the crushed roots, simmering 25 g (1 oz) crushed root in 1 litre (2 pints) cold water or milk until the liquid is reduced by 25 per cent. Take several wineglasses a day, but no more than 500 ml (1 pint) as a tonic. Leaves may also be used in an infusion of 25 g (1 oz) leaves to 500 ml (1 pint) of boiling water. Reputed to heel wounds and sooth stomach ulcers, the bowels, sore throats and bronchial infections.

Elecampane

Use the root, infusing 25 g (1 oz) root in 500 ml (1 pint) cold water brought to boiling point in a covered enamel pan. Take frequently in wineglassfuls for bronchial problems, coughing, hay fever, and urinary problems. The infusion is also antiseptic.

Horehound

Use leaf, stem or root, infusing 25 g (1 oz) in 500 ml (1 pint) boiling water. Take in teacupfuls often, up to 500 ml (1 pint) a day. This has a reputation for warding off volds if taken when the first symptoms appear, and is good for coughs. It is also meant to soothe the nerves. Horehound candy used to be a favourite sweetmeat for children.

Lemon Balm

Infuse 25 g (1 oz) leaves in 500 ml (1 pint) boiling water for 15 minutes. Drink frequently, up to 500 ml (1 pint) a day, as a tonic. Lemon balm is recommended as an aid to relaxation, and helps to reduce temperatures and alleviate toothache.

Lucerne

Infuse 1 teaspoon of dried leaves or 25 g (1 oz) fresh leaves in 500 ml (1 pint) boiling milk or water and take daily in wineglassfuls (up to 500 ml (1 pint) a day) as a tonic.

Mallow

The stems, leaves or roots can be used. Infuse 25 g (1 oz) of mallow in 500 ml (1 pint) boiling water and take frequently in wineglassfuls, up to 250 ml ($\frac{1}{2}$ pint) a day. It is reputed to build up resistance to disease and has general healing properties. Mallow is recommended for laryngitis and cystitis.

Mullein

Use the leaves and root and infuse 25 g (1 oz) mullein in 500 ml (1 pint) boiling water or milk. Take two or three wineglassfuls daily to ease lung ailments, soothe sore throats and induce sleep. Mullein may also be used for bathing red, tired or inflamed eyes.

Pennyroyal

Use leaves, flowers, stems and roots, making an infusion of 25 g (1 oz) pennyroyal to 500 ml (1 pint) boiling water. Take one or two teacups a day to soothe the nerves, relieve painful periods and lift depression. Pennyroyal should not be taken when pregnant.

Peppermint

Use roots, leaves, stems and flowers, and make an infusion of 25 g (1 oz) peppermint to 500 ml (1 pint) boiling water. Take in wineglassfuls as frequently as liked to aid digestion, calm the nerves and induce soothing sleep. Peppermint is reputed to aid those with migraine.

Red Clover

Infuse 25 g (1 oz) leaves and flowers in 500 ml (1 pint) boiling water. Drink frequently, but no more than 500 ml (1 pint) a day, as a gentle aid to constipation, and for inducing sound sleep.

Rue

Infuse 2 teaspoons chopped fresh leaves in 500 ml (1 pint) boiling water, and take 2 wineglassfuls daily. Recommended for strengthening eyesight, and for the veins and arteries, for reducing high blood pressure and easing cramp and painful periods. Rue should not be taken in large quantities or while pregnant.

Vervain

Infuse 25 g (1 oz) leaves and flowers in 500 ml (1 pint) boiling water, and take two or three wineglassfuls daily, up to 500 ml (1 pint) a day, as a tonic. Vervain is traditionally used to strengthen the heart, liver and spleen, lift depression, and cut infectious diseases. It makes a good gargle for sore throats, and a lotion for sore eyes.

Wild Parsley

Use leaves, stems and seeds, and infuse 25 g (1 oz) fresh herb or 1 heaped teaspoon of dried wild parsley in 500 ml (1 pint) boiling water. Take three or four wineglassfuls daily, up to 500 ml (1 pint) a day, as a tonic. Reputed to cure anaemia and difficult periods, and frequently used for rheumatism, sciatica and jaundice, as well as treating tumours and boils.

Yarrow

Use leaves, stems and flowers, and make an infusion of 25 g (1 oz) fresh or 1 teaspoon dried yarrow in 500 ml (1 pint) boiling water. Take two or three wineglassfuls a day. Relieves colds and flu quickly, and helps kidney disorders, corrects diarrhoea and purifies the blood.

Herb Teas

Many aromatic culinary herbs, infused and called *tisanes* are soothing to drink after meals or just before bedtime. They are particularly popular in France to purify the blood and aid digestion, as well as promoting soothing sleep and calming the nerves. Use mint, sage, lemon balm, marjoram, thyme, camomile, or lime flowers. These may be used fresh or dried and simply infused in boiling water before drinking. A little honey may be stirred in if a sweet drink is preferred.

Herb teas should be infused in earthenware or china or glass, but not in metals which affect their flavour. If the leaves are steeped for too long, the flavour will also be ruined; it is better to use more herbs and infuse them for a shorter time if a strong flavour is wanted. Use 1 teaspoon dried herbs for each cup of tea, with an extra teaspoon for the pot. If using herb seeds (e.g. the aniseed-flavoured herbs), allow 1 tablespoon seeds to each 500 ml (1 pint) of water, crushing the seeds slightly. If using fresh herb leaves, allow 3 teaspoons leaves for each cup of liquid, bruising the leaves slightly before infusing.

Herbs for Health

Honey Posset

500 ml (1 pint) milk
2 tablespoons honey
juice of 1 lemon

Bring the milk almost to the boil and stir in the honey and lemon juice. Boil gently until the curd separates. A nourishing dish for invalids.

Honey Cordial

1 tablespoon honey
juice of ½ lemon
boiling water

Put the honey and juice into a pottery mug and fill it up with hot water. Drink this to ease sore throats and to induce sleep. The addition of a little whisky or rum will induce even sounder sleep and help to drive out a cold.

Raspberry Vinegar

900 g (2 lb) raspberries
1 litre (2 pints) white vinegar
sugar

Cover the berries with vinegar and leave to stand for 4 days. Strain through a sieve without pressing the fruit. To each 500 ml (1 pint) of juice, allow 100 g (4 oz) sugar. Simmer gently together for 10 minutes and then bottle. This raspberry vinegar is a very old-fashioned mixture, used as a sauce over sweet puddings, or diluted with water to make a soothing drink for coughs and colds.

Inhaler for Colds

4 tablespoons peppermint leaves
4 tablespoons lime flowers
4 tablespoons camomile flowers
4 tablespoons sage leaves
1 litre (2 pints) boiling water

Mix the shredded peppermint leaves, whole lime and camomile flowers and shredded sage leaves. Pour on the boiling water and at once inhale the steam, with a towel over your head so the vapours don't escape, for 15 minutes. Stay indoors for an hour afterwards, or go straight to bed.

Mild Cough Mixture

175 g (6 oz) clear honey
juice of 2 lemons
50 g (2 oz) glycerine

Stir the honey, lemon juice and glycerine together until well mixed, bottle and cork firmly. A spoonful of this mixture will soothe a rough throat and ease a cough.

Chest Ointment

1 small head of garlic
1 jar Vaseline

Peel the garlic cloves and chop them very finely. Stir them into the Vaseline and leave in a warm place (such as an airing cupboard or the side of a solid-fuel cooker) for 7 days. Remove and leave to get cold. Massage the ointment generously into the chest and back to relieve tightness of the chest.

Bruise Oil

lemon balm leaves
rosemary leaves
camomile flowers
rosebuds
sage leaves
lavender flowers
southernwood leaves
wormwood leaves
salad oil

Take 4 tablespoons of each of the herb leaves and flowers and chop them up finely. Cover completely with salad oil and leave to stand for 14 days, stirring often. Boil very gently until the herbs become crisp and all their oils have been extracted, but do not let the oil get hotter than boiling water. Strain through a piece of clean fabric such as a handkerchief or old sheet into a clean bottle. Cork tightly until needed.

Cold Relief

Grate some fresh horseradish and inhale the fumes.

Headache Relief

Infuse 25 g (1 oz) rosemary flowers in 500 ml (1 pint) boiling water for 15 minutes. Cool and strain into a bottle. Drink a hot wineglassful four times daily.

Memory Strengthener

Infuse 25 g (1 oz) lemon balm in 500 ml (1 pint) boiling water for 15 minutes. Cool and bottle. Drink this often, with the addition of a little lemon juice and sugar.

Teeth Whitener

Rub the teeth with fresh sage leaves.

Wart Remover

Remove beans from broad bean pods and use the inside of the pods to rub the warts.

Rheumatism Reliever

Boil 25 g (1 oz) celery seed in 500 ml (1 pint) water until the liquid is reduced by half. Strain, bottle and cork tightly. Take 1 teaspoon of the mixture in a little water twice a day for 14 days.

To Ease Nettle Rash

Rub the rash with a little parsley to soothe the skin.

Honey for Skin Conditions

Scalds Honey on a clean dressing will relieve pain and encourage rapid healing.

Septic wounds Honey cleanses and heals when applied gently. Festering wounds which are swelling will be eased by honey which draws out the poisons and helps to form new healthy tissues. Deep cuts used to be treated quickly with an application of cobwebs to stop the bleeding, then a smear of honey before being tightly bound.

Skin irritations Itching and irritating skin rashes can be soothed by applying honey which will help to heal without leaving scars.

VEGETABLES FOR BEAUTY

All kinds of vegetables have beautifying properties when they are freshly picked. The fashionable white skin of the Victorians and Edwardians was improved by eating plenty of carrots and parsnips. Colourful cheeks are helped along by lettuce and watercress which supply iron, while a clear skin is promoted by spinach and onions which help to purify the blood. Fresh tomatoes cleanse the liver, but should not be eaten with vinegar for this purpose. Tomato juice removes stains from the hands, while a cucumber wash helps a sunburned or over-red face. Lettuce stalks contain a soporific, and a lettuce eaten with brown bread and butter before going to bed will ward off insomnia. Parsley aids digestion and also helps to promote a clear skin, so even the garnish of a dish is worth eating.

Cucumber Face Wash

2 cucumbers
eau de cologne

Cut the cucumbers into small pieces without peeling them, and mash to a pulp with a potato masher (or put in small quantities into a blender).

Simmer the pulp for 10 minutes and strain off the liquid. Add 1 tablespoon *eau de cologne* to each 500 ml (1 pint) of liquid and bottle. Use this face wash to sponge the face two or three times a day.

Herbal Hair Tonic

4 tablespoons rosemary or sage leaves
250 ml (¼ pint) cider vinegar
250 ml (¼ pint) water

Put the herbs into the vinegar and water and boil together for 5 minutes. Cool, strain and bottle. Apply to the scalp daily with cotton wool. Rosemary promotes growth, while sage is a tonic for the hair.

Marigold Skin Cleanser

250 ml (¼ pint) water
3 tablespoons marigold petals

Boil the water and add the marigold petals. Simmer for 5 minutes, cool, strain and bottle. This will keep for a week and should be rubbed into the skin to act as a moisturiser, skin tonic and softener.

Eye Soothers

Make up some strong camomile tea with camomile flowers, and wring out cotton wool pads in the tea. Put over closed eyes for 10 minutes.

To soothe and smooth the wrinkled skin round eyes, put freshly grated raw potatoes into a gauze pad and put this over the closed eyes for 10 minutes.

Honey for Hands

Rub honey on sore hands and cover with cotton gloves under rubber ones for housework to soothe cracks and soreness (honey makes a good facepack, too, mixed with a little oatmeal). For chapped hands, mix 100 g (4 oz) soft lard with 2 egg yolks, 2 tablespoons clear honey, 1 tablespoon ground almonds and 1 tablespoon rose-water, and a few drops of almond essence. Keep in a jar by the wash-basin and use constantly for healing and softening the hands.

Freckle Cleanser

clear honey
fennel seeds

Just warm the honey and stir in the crushed fennel to make a thick mixture. Spread on the face and leave for 15 minutes, then wash off with warm water.

Cold Cream

120 g (4½ oz) beeswax
175 g (6 oz) lard
175 g (6 oz) honey
a little essential oil

Melt the beeswax, lard and honey in a bowl standing in a pan of hot water. Remove from heat and stir until cool. Scent with a little essential oil of any desired perfume. (Tiny bottles of essential oils are obtainable in chemists, department stores and from herbalists for scenting beauty preparations and for *pot pourri*.)

Spot Soother

1 teaspoon honey
1 egg yolk
1 teaspoon yoghurt or sour milk

Mix all the ingredients well together and use on spots or blotches. Wash off with warm water.

Relaxing Bath Herbs

A warm bath containing herbs is a splendid relaxer for tired muscles. A selection of herbs may be put into small muslin bags for infusion in the warm water (the bags should be discarded after use, so it is worth making up a large supply of them for daily use). Make a mixture of mint, thyme, sage, rosemary, lavender, lemon balm, lemon verbena and camomile flowers and pack in bags the size of traditional lavender bags.

Flowers for Food and Scent

Flowers serve a double purpose in cookery, providing colour and delicacy of flavour, both of which were much appreciated by our Elizabethan ancestors. Early still-room books give recipes for candying borage, cowslips, marigolds, rosemary, roses and violets, as well as instructions for a variety of pastes, syrups and waters made from many flowers. In early days, many plants which we now regard purely as decorative flowers were also used as salad greens. The bright patch of nasturtiums, for instance, was used to provide colourful flowers to garnish dishes, the slightly bitter leaves were added to salads or eaten with brown bread, and the seeds were pickled as a relish. Borage, a little-used herb, gave the cucumber flavour of its leaves to long summer drinks, but its brilliant blue flowers were also a favourite garnish. Chrysanthemums used to be an ingredient in soups, broom buds made into pickles, and marrow flowers stuffed with meat and rice.

Rose geraniums, found on every cottage windowsill, were used for adding flavour to cooked apples, apple jelly and sponge cakes, but in this case the delicately scented flavour came from the leaves. One leaf should be placed at the bottom of each sponge tin before the batter is poured in, and should be removed before the cake is served. The leaves of lemon verbena can be used in the same way. Elderflowers have a wonderful muscat scent, and a head of flowers can be drawn through any fine jam or jelly just before bottling to give a delicate perfume.

Roses and violets are the most widely used flowers for both flavouring and decorative purposes in cooking, but lime leaves and blossoms have some unusual uses, while even marigolds, pansies, peonies and carnations have been used for their colour and flavour. Flower jams and jellies are particularly attractive to eat on biscuits and bread, or to eat with a spoon and a little cream.

Those who are less adventurous may prefer to concentrate on the scent rather than the flavour of flowers and leaves, and the making of *pot pourri* is a delightful occupation.

Carnation Syrup

1·5 litres (3 pints) carnation petals
2·5 litres (5 pints) boiling water
sugar

Pick the carnation heads, take off the white ends of the flowers, and then measure the petals. Pour boiling water over them and leave to stand for 12 hours. Strain off the liquid, but do not try to press out juice from the petals. Measure the liquid and allow 900 g (2 lb) sugar to every 500 ml (1 pint). Heat slowly to dissolve the sugar and simmer until the mixture is a light syrup. Put into bottles and cork tightly. Use to flavour drinks and fruit dishes, or as a sauce for mousses, ices or puddings.

Carnation Jam

225 g (8 oz) red carnation petals
250 ml (¼ pint) water
225 g (8 oz) sugar

Put the carnation petals into a bowl and crush them well with a wooden spoon. Mix together the water and sugar and heat gently until the sugar dissolves. Boil until the mixture is a thick syrup. Stir in the petals and simmer until the mixture forms a soft pulp. Put into small jars.

Carnation Butter

75 g (3 oz) unsalted butter
75 g (3 oz) red carnation petals

Cream the butter until it is soft and light. Put the carnation petals into a bowl and crush them well with a wooden spoon. Stir them into the butter and mix very well. Serve on small pieces of toast or in brown bread sandwiches.

Lavender Flavourings

Lavender tea may be made by pouring 500 ml (1 pint) boiling water on a tablespoon of young lavender leaves, infusing for 3 minutes, and serving hot or diced. The lavender flowers can be put in a single layer in jam jars, then topped with apple jelly and sealed when hot, for a delicious preserve.

Lavender Sugar

sprigs of fresh lavender
caster sugar

Clean the lavender sprigs by rinsing them in a little cold water, then leave them to stand until dry. Put into a screw-topped jar and fill with sugar. Shake well and leave for 24 hours. Shake well again and leave to stand for a week. Use to flavour milk puddings, or to sprinkle on cakes or biscuits.

Sprigs of rosemary may be used in the same way.

Lime Leaf Sandwiches

The leaves of lime trees can be used for flavouring while the pink scales still cling to the leaf buds. Cut the leaves from the stalks with scissors, and rinse them well in running water. Use them chopped and tossed in lemon juice in white bread and butter sandwiches, or substitute salt, pepper and cream for the lemon juice. For brown bread sandwiches, the lime leaves can be chopped and mixed with cream cheese.

Lime Blossom Tea

This is a great favourite in France, known as *Tilleul* and usually drunk just before bedtime to induce relaxation and sound sleep. Gather the lime flowers in July and dry them lightly. They should be picked when the dew has dried, and then spread in a single layer on baking sheets and left in a dry place away from bright sunlight until just crisp. If preferred, they may be dried in an airing cupboard or very low oven. Use a small handful of flowers in a medium-sized pot with boiling water for a beautifully scented China-type tea. Store the flowers in a jar or tin.

Marigold Flavourings

Marigold petals were traditionally sprinkled on salads and cold meat dishes. Their flavour and colour can be used for cakes and custards if the petals are put into a small muslin bag and infused in a small cup of hot milk, which can then be used for recipes.

Marigold Conserve

150 g (5 oz) marigold petals
lemon juice
450 g (1 lb) sugar

Use the old-fashioned pot marigolds for this recipe. Mash the petals with a wooden spoon, or use a blender on low speed. Add a little lemon juice to help the mashing process. Gradually work in the sugar until it is completely absorbed and put into small jars. Store in a cool place.

Marigold Eggs

4 eggs
4 tablespoons milk
salt and pepper
pinch nutmeg
25 g (1 oz) butter
2 marigold heads
toast

Beat the eggs and milk together lightly and season with salt, pepper and nutmeg. Melt the butter and stir in the egg mixture. Cook over a low heat, stirring occasionally, until just set. Remove the petals from the marigold heads, wash and pat dry, and chop finely, reserving a few petals for garnish. Stir into the eggs, and serve on buttered toast, garnishing with a few petals.

Marigolds and eggs seem to go well together. In earlier days they were added to an egg custard which was poured over sliced apples and baked in a pastry flan as a traditional accompaniment to roast pork.

Marigold Potato Salad

675 g (1¼ lb) potatoes
250 ml (½ pint) mayonnaise
1 bunch watercress
3 marigold heads
2 tablespoons chives

Use rather 'waxy' potatoes if possible, so that they do not become mushy when tossed in the dressing. Cook the potatoes, cut them in cubes and toss in the mayonnaise while still slightly warm. Chop the watercress and stir it in. Garnish with marigold petals and chopped chives.

Nasturtium Flavourings

Nasturtium leaves contain ten times as much vitamin C as lettuce, and can be used in salads and sandwiches. The flowers look good on both vegetable and fruit salads, and can be minced and mixed with cream cheese or butter. The seeds can be pickled (see page 100), or dried and ground as a fiery pepper. The pickled seeds can be used as capers in white sauce to serve with lamb. Use the flowers in the same way as marigolds for potato salad, with the addition of a few green nasturtium seeds and one or two chopped leaves, or fry the flowers lightly in butter and add to a clear chicken soup.

Peony Flavourings

Peony kernels used to be dried and powdered to use like pepper. The kernels can also be used to decorate cakes and puddings in the same way as almonds. An infusion of peony flowers (without the green calyx) was made and sweetened with honey as a health-giving drink in the seventeenth and eighteenth centuries. To make this, leave 1 litre (2 pints) of peony flowers in enough wine to cover for 24 hours, then drain them and boil the flowers with 1 litre (2 pints) water, simmering for 10 minutes. Strain the liquid, sweeten with honey and add to the drained wine.

Primrose Flavourings

Primroses are a delightful addition to spring menus. Disraeli, founder of the Primrose League, used to eat young shoots of primroses which had been soaked in salted water, drained and boiled in fresh water for 10 minutes, and then drained again and dressed in oil and vinegar sauce, with primrose petals to garnish. Primroses were also mixed with sugar, dried fruit and nuts as a favourite filling for a suet pudding. The flowers can be dipped in a thin batter and fried, or simply fried in butter and dressed with sugar and orange juice. A creamy rice pudding, sweetened with honey and flavoured with cinnamon, is delicious if a few bruised primrose petals are added, and primrose petals are sprinkled over as a garnish before serving.

Rose Flavourings

There must be hundreds of ways of using roses in cooking, and many of these are still practised all over the world. The best kind of cooking roses are the old-fashioned, heavily-scented varieties which have been traditionally used for jams and jellies, wines and syrups and delicate puddings. Country people would put a handful of rose petals under the crust of a cherry or plum pie. Another favourite dish was rose petals dipped first in brandy, then in melted butter and quickly fried before being dusted with caster sugar. Tight rose buds used to be pickled in a syrup of 1 part sugar to 4 parts white wine vinegar, and after storing for 1 month, the buds were used in salads and sandwiches, and with cold meat.

Rose Honey

225 g (8 oz) rose petals
500 ml (1 pint) water
900 g (2 lb) clear honey

Remove the white ends from the rose petals, and mash the petals with a wooden spoon. Boil for 15 minutes in the water. Add the honey and boil gently to a thick syrup. Pour into small jars and cover.

Rose Petal Conserve

450 g (1 lb) sugar
1 tablespoon water
450 g (1 lb) dark red rose petals
1 dessertspoon orange flower or rose-water

Boil the sugar and water slowly to make a syrup. Wash and dry the flower petals and stir them into the syrup with the orange flower or rose-water. Simmer to a thick syrup and pour into small jars. The mixture will not set.

Rose Petal Jam (1)

450 g (1 lb) dark red rose petals
450 g (1 lb) sugar
125 ml (¼ pint) rose-water
1 tablespoon orange flower water

Spread the petals to dry in a light draught but away from direct sunlight. Put them into a strainer and dip in boiling water for a second, then drain and dry petals. Heat sugar, rose-water and orange flower water gently to make a light syrup. Add the rose petals and simmer for 45 minutes, stirring occasionally, until the mixture is soft and thick. Pour into small jars.

Rose Petal Jam (2)

450 g (1 lb) dark red rose petals
675 g (1½ lb) sugar
250 ml (½ pint) water
juice of ½ lemon

Snip the white bases from the petals and cut the petals into pieces which are not too small. Put them into a basin with half the sugar, cover and leave to stand for 48 hours. Dissolve the remaining sugar in the water and lemon juice, then stir in the rose petals and bring to the boil. Simmer for 20 minutes until the jam thickens. Pour into small jars and cover.

Rose Petal and Rhubarb Jam

450 g (1 lb) rhubarb
juice of 1 lemon
450 g (1 lb) sugar
100 g (4 oz) dark red rose petals

Prepare the rhubarb and leave overnight with the lemon juice and sugar. Next day, cut the rose petals in pieces and add to the mixture. Bring to the boil, and boil to setting point. Pour into small hot jars and cover.

Rose Petal Jelly

rose petals
apple juice (see method)
sugar

The white 'heels' of the petals should be cut away, and the petals should be dried in a slight draught, away from direct sunshine. Cut up some unpeeled cooking apples in small pieces and cover with cold water. Simmer to a pulp, and strain through a jelly bag overnight. Allow 450 g (1 lb) sugar to 500 ml (1 pint) liquid, and stir over low heat until the sugar has dissolved. Add as many dried rose petals as the liquid will hold, and boil until the jelly sets on a cold plate. Strain and pour into warm jars. The jelly has the colour and scent of roses.

Rose Petal Ice

1 litre (2 pints) water
450 g (1 lb) caster sugar
2 teaspoons grated lemon rind
125 ml ($\frac{1}{4}$ pint) lemon juice
2 tablespoons rose petal jam (page 146)

Mix together all the ingredients very thoroughly and bring to the boil, stirring well. Cool and put into freezer trays in the ice compartment of the refrigerator at the lowest setting. Freeze for an hour until the mixture is mushy. Put into a chilled bowl, beat well and return to the freezer tray. Cover with foil and freeze for 2 hours. Serve in small glasses with thin sweet biscuits. If liked, garnish with a few crystallised rose petals.

Rose Mousse

6 egg whites
6 tablespoons rose petal jam (page 146)
2 tablespoons fruit brandy (apricot or raspberry)

Beat the egg whites to stiff peaks, gradually whisking in the rose petal jam. Fold in the brandy and turn into a soufflé dish which has been buttered and dusted with caster sugar. Bake at 200°C (400°F)/Gas 6 for 10 minutes and serve at once.

Violet Flavourings

Violets are second only to roses as popular culinary flowers. The flowers may be used in a potato salad dressed with oil and vinegar, and candied violets can be folded into all sorts of puddings to give a delicate flavour. Violets were particularly popular with the Victorians and Edwardians who loved them in creams, ices and mousses.

Violet Ice Cream

> 250 ml ($\frac{1}{2}$ pint) double cream
> 50 g (2 oz) soft brown breadcrumbs
> 100 g (4 oz) demerara sugar
> 100 g (4 oz) candied violets (page 149)

Whip the cream to soft peaks and fold in the breadcrumbs, sugar and half the violets crushed with a rolling pin. Put into a freezer tray and freeze in the ice compartment of the refrigerator at the lowest setting for 1 hour. Put into a chilled bowl and beat until soft. Return to the freezer tray, cover with foil and freeze for 2 hours. Scoop out into small bowls and sprinkle with the remaining violets.

Violet Mousse

> 125 ml ($\frac{1}{4}$ pint) water
> 50 g (2 oz) sugar
> 50 g (2 oz) violet petals
> 4 eggs, separated
> 125 ml ($\frac{1}{4}$ pint) double cream
> 50 g (2 oz) candied violets (page 149)

Boil the water and stir in the sugar until it has dissolved. Simmer to a thin syrup and pour over the violet petals. Leave to stand for 10 minutes. Strain and put the liquid into a double saucepan, or into a bowl over a pan of hot water. Add the egg yolks one at a time, and stir over the hot water until the mixture is thick. Cool slightly and then fold into the softly-whipped cream. Whisk the egg whites to stiff peaks, and fold into the violet mixture. Pour into a serving bowl and chill for 3 hours. Decorate with candied violets just before serving.

Violet Jam

225 g (8 oz) violet flowers
500 ml (1 pint) boiling water
675 g (1½ lb) sugar

Put three-quarters of the flowers into a bowl and cover with boiling water. Cover and leave for 15 hours. Strain the liquid through a jelly bag. Add the sugar and stir until dissolved. Bring to the boil, add the remaining flowers, and boil to setting point. Pour into small jars and cover.

Conserve of Flowers

225 g (8 oz) flower petals (carnations, jasmine, primroses, violets, roses)
1·8 kg (4 lb) cooking apples
1 litre (2 pints) water
sugar

Choose the flowers according to the season of the year. Cut the fruit in pieces and put into a preserving pan with the water and flower petals. Simmer until the fruit is pulpy, and strain through a jelly bag. Measure the juice and allow 450 g (1 lb) sugar to each 500 ml (1 pint) juice. Stir in the sugar until dissolved, boil rapidly to setting point, and put into small jars.

Flower Vinegars

Vinegar flavoured with flowers was made until the middle of the nineteenth century, for use as toilet waters, but also for dressing salads and for diluting as drinks. A tablespoon of flower vinegar in iced water, sweetened with honey, is delicious and soothing. Roses, clove pinks, lavender, rosemary and violets were particularly popular, either singly or combined. One part lavender to four parts rose petals makes a good mixture, or equal parts of clove pinks, rose petals, rosemary and elderflowers.

To make flower vinegar, use 250 ml (½ pint) petals without white bases and put them into a preserving jar. Cover with a 500 ml (1 pint) of boiling white vinegar and cover tightly. Leave for 10 days in a warm place, shaking the jar once a day. If the flavour is not strong enough after this time, strain the liquid from the flowers, add another 250 ml (½ pint) of fresh flowers and leave for another 10 days. Strain through muslin and put into glass bottles.

Candied Roses and Violets

225 g (8 oz) rose petals or violets
100 ml (4 fl oz) water
225 g (8 oz) granulated sugar

The flowers should be gathered early when the dew has just dried. Bring the water to the boil and remove from the heat. Stir in the sugar until dissolved. Remove the stems from the flowers, and lightly wash and drain them without bruising in a colander. Put the syrup back on the heat and stir in the flowers. Cook gently to 115°C (240°F) (soft ball). Take off the heat and stir with a wooden spoon until the syrup begins to granulate to the texture of coarse meal. Pour the contents of the pan into a colander and shake off the extra sugar as the flowers cool. Store in jars with the lids sealed with sticky tape.

Crystallised Flowers

A variety of crystallised flowers can be made for cake decorations or small sweets. The flowers will last several months and keep their natural colours. Suitable flowers are primroses, violets, polyanthus, roses, carnation petals, forget-me-nots, mimosa, cowslips, sweet peas, and fruit blossoms. Flowers which come from bulbs should not be eaten.

The flowers are crystallised in a solution of gum Arabic crystals and rose or orange flower water. Allow 3 teaspoons crystals to 3 tablespoons rose-water, and leave in a screwtop jar for two or three days, shaking sometimes, until the mixture is a sticky glue. A small soft paint brush is needed to paint the flowers. Large flowers should be taken apart and the petals re-assembled when needed. The petals must be completely coated, or bare spots will shrivel and not keep. A little vegetable colouring may be added to the solution, but this must be very delicate to remain natural. When the flowers have been sugared, they should be dried for about 24 hours until crisp and dry. They are best stored in the dark. For short-term use, flowers can be quickly crystallised with beaten egg white and sugar, but they will not store for long.

Pot Pourri

Pot pourri is a mixture of dried flowers, leaves and spices. The secret of success lies in the choice of scents, in correct drying methods, and in the use of the right container. *Pot pourri* can be used in small quantities to fill muslin bags or cushions, but it is more commonly kept in a jar. The jar needs a well-fitting lid and a stand, and special jars were once made for this purpose. Try a ginger jar, with a wooden lid and stand. The *pot pourri* should be kept in the tightly closed jar all day, and in the evening should be turned till pleasantly warm, moved to its stand and left to cool, when the scent will fill the room. When cool, replace the lid till further use.

Roses are the traditional floral ingredient of *pot pourri*, but other flowers can be used to give colour and variety to the mixture. The flowers should be gathered freshly after the dew has dried, and should not have fully blossomed, as their scent is strongest then. They must be dried, the scents fixed, and the blossoms blended with appropriate leaves, herbs and spices.

A box of fine sand is needed for drying the flowers. The petals should be placed on a layer of sand, then sprinkled with more sand, and so on in layers till the box is full, care being taken not to put too many petals into one box as they may mildew. The sand boxes without lids should be kept in a warm dry place away from sunlight and draughts, and after a few days they will be crisp and retain their shape and colour. Different types of flowers and scented leaves should be kept in separate boxes. When they are ready for use, the sand can be sifted away. Flowers gathered at various times can be kept dried till the time comes to blend them.

If an extra fragrant mixture is required, the petals can be sealed, after drying, into jars with 2 tablespoons of kitchen salt. They should be left to stand for 3 weeks before mixing together. As a final fixative, powdered orris root is used. When the flowers, spices and fixatives have been mixed they should be sealed into jars or packets as required.

Mixture 1

In a bowl, put alternate layers of rose petals, bayleaves and the powdered rind of two oranges, sprinkling each layer with a mixture of equal parts powdered cloves, allspice, cinnamon and mace. Finish with a layer of rose petals and a scattering of lavender flowers.

Mixture 2

Use alternate layers of lavender, lemon balm, thyme and mint, sprinkling each layer with a mixture of cloves and cinnamon. Leave for a few days before stirring and mixing together.

Mixture 3

Mix 1 litre (2 pints) of rose petals with a cup of marjoram, lemon, thyme, rosemary and lavender. Sprinkle with the powdered rind of an orange and a lemon, 6 broken bayleaves, 1 tablespoon cloves and 1 teaspoon allspice.

Old Hall Pot Pourri

900 g (2 lb) red rose petals
225 g (8 oz) lemon verbena leaves
225 g (8 oz) rose geranium leaves
225 g (8 oz) lavender leaves
225 g (8 oz) rosemary leaves
1 dessertspoon marjoram
1 dessertspoon lemon thyme

1 dessertspoon orris root powder
1 dessertspoon gum benzoin
1 dessertspoon ground allspice
1 dessertspoon ground cloves
pinch nutmeg
1 teaspoon dried orange peel
1 teaspoon dried lemon peel
10 drops rose oil
3 drops rosemary oil

If the summer is hot and dry, the petals and leaves can be simply spread out on cake racks and left to dry in a shady dry place in the house. Put each type of petal or leaf in a separate container until ready to mix. When all the leaves and flowers are dry and crisp, put into a large cake tin or polythene box and add the orris root, gum benzoin, spices, peels and oils. Keep tightly covered for six weeks, stirring occasionally, before putting into jars. This gives a beautifully scented mixture with a pretty contrast of colours. Orris root, ground spices and dried fruit peels can be bought in many chemists and stores. Essential oils may also be bought to boost the scent of *pot pourri*.

Lavender Sticks

Lavender sticks were used to mark the dozens and half-dozens in our grandmothers' trousseau chests, and they keep their fragrance for years. For each stick, take a small bunch of lavender and a length of narrow baby ribbon. Pick the lavender blooms on a fine day, and use them while the stems are still supple. Take an odd number of stems (13 gives a satisfactory 'stick') and tie them firmly together with one end of the ribbon immediately below the flower heads. Turn the bunch upside down and carefully bend the stalks out and over the heads from the point where the ribbon is tied so that the heads appear to be in a cage of stems. Space the stalks evenly, and then starting at the top where the stalks bend, weave the long end of the ribbon over and under the stalks so that the flower heads become completely enclosed in a kind of basketwork of ribbon and stalk. Make the weaving rather tight at the bottom and top of the heads and rather slacker in the centre to give a 'bottle appearance'. When the heads are completely covered, wind the ribbon firmly round the stalks for 2·5–5 cm (1–2 in), then tie in a bow. Leave about 7·5 cm (3 in) of stalk below this bow, and trim neatly to an even length with sharp scissors.

Scented Pillows

Sleep sweetly on scented silk or satin pillows stuffed with *pot pourri* mixture. Try well-dried rose petals mixed with a teaspoon each of powdered dried mint and powdered cloves. Or try equal quantities of lavender, lemon verbena and rose scented geranium leaves, with a teaspoon each of powdered orris root and cinnamon.

Fragrance for Linen

Fill small muslin bags with equal quantities of rosemary, thyme and bay-leaves, rubbed small. Or try 2 parts each of powdered mint and rosemary to one part of thyme, tansy and powdered cloves.

Honey, Yoghurt, Eggs and Bread

As soon as a family becomes used to the idea that so many marvellous fruits and vegetables can be grown even in a limited space, and that their quality and flavour are unbeatable, thoughts begin to turn to other kinds of home food production. Few people have the space to keep a house cow or grow several acres of cereals, but everyone can use bought raw materials to produce their own rightly-flavoured and textured yoghurt and bread as an alternative to the bland shop varieties. Bees and chickens present few problems and do not require much work, and there is little to equal the satisfaction of gathering and using home-produced honey and eggs.

HONEY

Honey is a delicious, pure and healthy food. It is very easily digested and absorbed into the bloodstream quickly, which makes it useful in restoring energy. A piece of wholemeal bread spread with butter and honey is a really quick 'pick-me-up', and so is a glass of hot water with the juice of a lemon well-sweetened with honey. Because of these qualities, honey is particularly good for children, old people and invalids, and it is easy to use as a sweetener for a glass of milk, citrus fruit, stewed fruit, baked apples or fruit salad. When it is used in this way, substitute 1 tablespoon honey for $1\frac{1}{2}$ tablespoons sugar.

When honey is substituted for sugar in cooking, measurements must be adjusted, as honey has almost twice the sweetness of sugar. It is not advisable to substitute honey for more than one-third of the sugar in a cake or biscuit recipe, as this can result in too much browning. When adapting ordinary sugar-based recipes for baking, use three-quarters of the stated amount of sugar and one-quarter honey, but reduce the liquid in the recipe by 3 tablespoons for each 225 g (8 oz) honey used. A small pinch of bicarbonate of soda will neutralise the effects of the acids in the honey.

Liquify the honey before use by standing the jar in a pan of very hot water, but do not overheat, as this affects the flavour. To ease mixing, the honey can be blended with the other liquids before it is added to the bulk of the recipe. Cakes and biscuits made with honey will have a chewy texture and be browner, and they will also keep moist longer. When measuring honey, heat the tablespoon in hot water and dry quickly before scooping the honey; a tablespoon equals 25 g (1 oz).

Honey is also delicious as a quick topping for plain cakes. Try spreading a spongecake thinly with honey, and sprinkling with chopped nuts or desiccated coconut. A creamy filling or icing can be made using a proportion of 50 g (2 oz) butter to 25 g (1 oz) honey. Equal quantities of honey and butter creamed together can be served as Honey Butter with scones, teacakes or wholemeal bread. Honey blends well with a number of flavours for sandwiches—try honey and chopped nuts or mashed bananas, or honey with chopped apple and dried fruit, particularly dates.

If you have a large supply of honey, you may want to try using it for preserving. It affects the flavour of both bottled and frozen fruit, but this is a matter of personal preference. It gives a good flavour to jams, but prevents firm setting, and should only be used in the proportion of one-quarter or one-half honey to sugar.

Honey Bran Muffins

100 g (4 oz) plain flour
2 teaspoons baking powder
½ teaspoon salt
40 g (1½ oz) lard
50 g (2 oz) bran cereal
50 g (2 oz) chopped nuts
1 egg
100 ml (4 fl oz) milk
8 tablespoons honey

Sift together the flour, baking powder and salt. Lightly rub in the lard and stir in the cereal and nuts. Mix in the egg, beaten with the milk and honey, and divide the mixture into deep greased patty tins. Bake at 220°C

(425°F)/Gas 7 for 20 minutes. Serve freshly baked with butter for spreading.

Honey Date Bars

75 g (3 oz) butter
100 g (4 oz) honey
1 teaspoon vanilla essence
3 eggs
175 g (6 oz) plain flour
1 teaspoon baking powder
½ teaspoon salt
175 g (6 oz) chopped dates
100 g (4 oz) chopped nuts

Cream together the butter, honey and essence and beat in the eggs one at a time. Mix in the flour, sieved with baking powder and salt, and then add the dates and nuts. Spread on a greased baking sheet about 23 × 30 cm (9 × 12 in) and bake at 180°C (350°F)/Gas 4 for 30 minutes. Cool, cut into bars and sprinkle with a little icing sugar.

Honey Spiced Biscuits

75 g (3 oz) butter
50 g (2 oz) sugar
3 tablespoons honey
1 egg
225 g (8 oz) plain flour
½ teaspoon salt
1 teaspoon bicarbonate of soda
1 teaspoon ground ginger
1 teaspoon ground cinnamon
125 ml (¼ pint) sour milk

Cream together the butter, sugar and honey and gradually work in the egg. Add the flour sifted with salt, soda and spices, and the milk, and mix to a firm dough. Drop in teaspoonfuls on a greased baking sheet and bake at 190°C (375°F)/Gas 5 for 10 minutes. Cool on a wire rack.

Honey Spice Cake

50 g (2 oz) butter
150 g (5 oz) honey
150 g (5 oz) demerara sugar
275 g (10 oz) plain flour

pinch salt
1 teaspoon bicarbonate of soda
1 teaspoon ground mixed spice
1 teaspoon ground ginger
1 teaspoon ground cinnamon
100 g (4 oz) chopped mixed candied peel
1 egg
125 ml (¼ pint) milk
25 g (1 oz) flaked almonds

Heat the butter gently until melted, then take it off the heat and stir in the honey and sugar. Stir well and cool. Sieve together the flour, salt, soda and spices and stir in the peel. Beat the egg and milk together and add to the cooled honey, then pour into the flour and beat until smooth. Pour into a greased and lined 450-g (1-lb) loaf tin and scatter the flaked almonds on top. Bake at 180°C (350°F)/Gas 4 for 1¼ hours. Cool and serve sliced and spread with butter.

Honey Fruit

4 eating apples or pears
4 tablespoons lemon juice
175 g (6 oz) honey
1 teaspoon ground cinnamon
25 g (1 oz) butter

If preferred, 675 g (1½ lb) sliced rhubarb can be substituted for the apples or pears, and either cinnamon or ginger used.

Wipe the apples and core them. If pears are to be used, peel and core them, and cut them in half. Arrange the fruit close together in a greased shallow ovenware dish, mix the lemon juice and honey, and pour over the fruit. Sprinkle with cinnamon, and dot with pieces of butter. Bake at 180°C (350°F)/Gas 4 for 25 minutes, and serve hot with cream.

Honey Junket

1 tablespoon clear honey
500 ml (1 pint) milk
2 drops vanilla essence
3 teaspoons rennet
pinch ground nutmeg

Warm the honey gently until runny. Add the milk and essence and heat until the milk is lukewarm. The milk should not be hotter than 38°C (100°F). Stir in the rennet and pour into a serving bowl. Leave in a warm place until set, and then chill the junket. Sprinkle with nutmeg just before serving. A Devonshire junket is traditionally covered with a layer of thick unwhipped cream just before serving.

Honey Cheesecake

225 g (8 oz) shortcrust pastry
225 g (8 oz) cottage cheese
100 g (4 oz) honey
100 g (4 oz) caster sugar
4 eggs
pinch ground cinnamon

Line a pie-plate or flan dish with the pastry. Prick the pastry with a fork and bake 'blind' at 200°C (400°F)/Gas 6 for 15 minutes. Sieve the cottage cheese and blend with the honey, sugar, beaten eggs and cinnamon. Fill the partly-baked pastry case with this mixture and bake at 190°C (375°F)/Gas 5 for 30 minutes. Sprinkle with a little more cinnamon when cooked.

Honey Pots

½ lemon
250 ml (½ pint) double cream
3 tablespoons clear honey
65 ml (2¼ fl oz) sherry or white wine
50 g (2 oz) toasted almonds or hazelnuts

Grate the lemon rind into a bowl and add the lemon juice. Add the cream, honey and sherry or wine. Whisk until thick and creamy and spoon into individual glasses or small bowls. Sprinkle with toasted almonds or hazelnuts.

Honey Ice Cream

450 g (1 lb) raspberries
125 ml (¼ pint) double cream
125 ml (¼ pint) natural yoghurt
10 tablespoons clear honey
2 tablespoons lemon juice
pinch salt
4 egg whites

Sieve the raspberries and put the purée into a bowl with the cream, yoghurt, honey, lemon juice and salt. Mix very well and pour into freezing trays. Cover with foil and freeze at the lowest setting in the freezer compartment of your refrigerator until the mixture is a softly-frozen mush.

Return to the mixing bowl and stir the mixture until smooth. Whisk the egg whites to stiff peaks and fold them into the raspberry mixture. Return to the freezer trays and freeze for 2 hours. Spoon into chilled glasses to serve.

Steamed Honey Pudding

50 g (2 oz) butter
50 g (2 oz) honey
1 egg
175 g (6 oz) plain flour
1 teaspoon baking powder
pinch salt
milk
50 g (2 oz) seedless raisins
2 drops lemon essence

For the sauce:
50 g (2 oz) honey
125 ml ($\frac{1}{4}$ pint) water
2 teaspoons lemon juice
1 teaspoon cornflour

Cream together the butter and honey and beat in the egg. Add the flour, sieved with the baking powder and salt, and mix to a dropping consistency with a little milk. Stir in the raisins and lemon essence. Put into a greased 500-ml (1-pint) pudding basin, cover with foil and steam for $1\frac{1}{2}$ hours.

Just before serving, make the sauce by mixing the honey, water, lemon juice and cornflour, bringing to the boil and simmering for 3 minutes. Turn out the pudding on a warm serving plate, pour over a little of the sauce, and serve the remaining sauce separately.

YOGHURT

Yoghurt is a marvellous natural food which originally came from Bulgaria, where it is reputed to be responsible for the large number of healthy elderly citizens. It is rich in vitamins A and D, has about 6 per cent protein, and is low in fat and calories. Yoghurt is made with fresh whole milk, skimmed milk, or either of these with dried milk added, giving a protein bonus due to the addition of non-fat solids. When cultures are added to the milk, lactic acid is produced. This aids digestion, and is particularly useful in the assimilation of calcium, essential to the growth and strengthening of teeth and bones. Both bought and home-made yoghurt requires a living bacteria which stays alive but remains dormant when kept at a low temperature.

This bacteria can die through age or heat, and then harmful bacteria take over and make the yoghurt unfit for consumption.

Natural yoghurt is delicious to eat on its own, or with fruit. The Scandinavians like it with brown sugar and cinnamon, accompanied by thin crisp ginger biscuits. It is also a most useful cooking ingredient, making a thick creamy sauce for meat, fish, poultry and curried dishes. If it is added towards the end of cooking, the result will be smooth and creamy, with a slight tang. It is good stirred into a pan of minced beef until heated through, or it can be added to the pan juices used in cooking liver or kidneys. Baked fish is creamy and has a delicious flavour if cooked in yoghurt, or the yoghurt can be used in a sauce for grilled or steamed fish.

Young carrots, spinach, broccoli and baby turnips are good when they are cooked in a little stock, or in a casserole with a little butter, with yoghurt added just before serving. A quick sauce can be made by flavouring yoghurt with fresh herbs, or with chopped capers or gherkins. A delicious potato salad is easily made by tossing potatoes in natural yoghurt with finely chopped onion and plenty of salt and pepper. Yoghurt is also excellent for baking and for making a variety of sweet dishes.

It is easy to make yoghurt at home with pasteurised, sterilised or Channel Islands milk, and the Milk Marketing Board recommends Ultra Heat Treated (UHT) Milk for a firmer texture. If you like flavoured yoghurt, stir in small pieces of fresh or thawed frozen fruit when the mixture has set.

Home-made Soft Yoghurt

500 ml (1 pint) milk
125 ml (¼ pint) natural yoghurt

Warm the milk to 42°C (106°F) and remove from the heat. Gently stir in the yoghurt with a wire whisk or fork. Transfer to a bowl and cover with a plate. Leave in a warm place for 8 to 12 hours until set, and then refrigerate before serving. If you prefer to make individual pots of yoghurt, this quantity will fill five 100-ml (4-fl oz) jars or bottles. The ideal temperature in which to set the yoghurt is 15°C (60°F). For a second batch, some home-made yoghurt can be used with fresh milk in the same proportions as above.

Breakfast Starter

1 grapefruit
1 tablespoon honey
125 ml (¼ pint) natural yoghurt

Peel the grapefruit and remove the segments carefully, discarding all the skin and pith. Mix with the honey and yoghurt and chill before serving.

Muesli

125 ml (¼ pint) natural yoghurt
juice of ½ lemon
2 tablespoons clear honey
8 tablespoons porridge oats
1 eating apple
25 g (1 oz) chopped mixed nuts
25 g (1 oz) raisins or sultanas

Mix the yoghurt, lemon juice and honey. Add the oats, chopped apple, nuts and raisins or sultanas and mix thoroughly. Leave to stand overnight. It is possible to buy bags of mixed prepared cereals for muesli. Some of these already have dried fruit and nuts added. If using these, simply add the yoghurt, lemon juice, honey and chopped fresh fruit and leave to stand overnight.

Yoghurt and Cucumber Soup

1 large cucumber
salt and pepper
250 ml (½ pint) natural yoghurt
chopped chives
chopped parsley
125 ml (¼ pint) milk

Wipe the cucumber and cut off a few thin slices for garnish. Grate the remainder coarsely into a bowl, sprinkle lightly with salt, and leave to stand for 5 minutes. Add pepper, yoghurt, and plenty of chives and parsley, and thin with the milk. Chill and serve in individual bowls garnished with cucumber slices.

Chicken Curry

1 small chicken
plain flour
salt and pepper
ground ginger
100 g (4 oz) butter
3 medium-sized onions
900 g (2 lb) tomatoes
1 tablespoon curry powder
250 ml (½ pint) natural yoghurt
50 g (2 oz) blanched almonds

Cut the chicken into four pieces and dip them in flour seasoned with salt and pepper. Sprinkle generously with ground ginger and fry in butter until the chicken pieces are well-browned. Take out the chicken pieces and put them into a casserole. Peel and slice the onions and fry them in the butter until soft and golden. Peel and slice the tomatoes and add to the onions. Cook for 5 minutes, stir in the curry powder, cook for 3 more minutes and then add the yoghurt. Mix well and pour over the chicken pieces. Cover and bake at 180°C (350°F)/Gas 4 for 30 minutes. Serve hot, sprinkled with almonds, with accompanying rice and chutney.

Yoghurt Salad Dressing

125 ml (¼ pint) natural yoghurt
juice of ½ lemon
salt and pepper
1 tablespoon parsley

Mix together the yoghurt and lemon juice and season well with salt and pepper. Add very finely chopped parsley. Serve on all types of salads.

Sweet Yoghurt Dressing

2 tablespoons honey
1 tablespoon lemon juice
250 ml (½ pint) natural yoghurt
1 teaspoon grated lemon rind
1 tablespoon orange juice

Stir together the honey and lemon juice until they are completely mixed. Beat the yoghurt very lightly and gradually add the honey and other ingredients. Chill and serve on fruit salads.

Yoghurt Herb Sauce

125 ml (¼ pint) natural yoghurt
1 teaspoon parsley
1 teaspoon chives
½ teaspoon thyme
salt and pepper

Put the yoghurt into a bowl and work in the very finely chopped fresh herbs and seasoning. Serve over new potatoes, carrots, broad beans, broccoli or cauliflower.

Yoghurt Scones

225 g (8 oz) plain flour
½ teaspoon salt
1¼ teaspoons baking powder
25 g (1 oz) butter
125 ml (¼ pint) natural yoghurt

Wholemeal flour or white flour may be used for these scones. Sift together the flour, salt and baking powder, and rub in the butter. Stir in the yoghurt to make a soft dough. Knead lightly until smooth. Roll out to a thickness of 1 cm (½ in) and cut into 5-cm (2-in) rounds. Put on to a greased baking sheet and bake at 200°C (400°F)/Gas 6 for 12 minutes. Cool on a wire rack. Serve split and buttered, or with jam and cream.

Yoghurt Gingerbread

100 g (4 oz) butter
50 g (2 oz) light soft brown sugar
50 g (2 oz) black treacle
175 g (6 oz) golden syrup
125 ml (¼ pint) natural yoghurt
2 eggs
225 g (8 oz) plain flour
1 teaspoon ground mixed spice
3 teaspoons ground ginger
½ teaspoon bicarbonate of soda

Put the butter, sugar, treacle and syrup into a thick saucepan and heat gently until the butter has melted and the sugar dissolved. Cool and stir in the yoghurt and beaten eggs. Sift together the flour, spices and soda and pour in the yoghurt mixture. Mix very thoroughly and put into a greased and lined 17·5-cm (7-in) square tin. Bake at 150°C (300°F)/Gas 2 for 1½ hours. Cool and store in an airtight tin. This gingerbread is best when it has been stored for at least 24 hours.

Yoghurt Fruit Fool

675 g (1½ lb) raspberries
a little sugar or honey
125 ml (¼ pint) double cream
125 ml (¼ pint) natural yoghurt
grated rind of 1 orange

Sieve the raspberries and sweeten them with a little sugar or honey if necessary. Whip the cream until just soft and beat in the yoghurt. Fold in

163

the raspberry purée and orange rind, and chill before serving. This is also good made with blackcurrants, which should be simmered in a little water before sieving and sweetening.

Blackberry and Apple Ice

375 ml ($\frac{3}{4}$ pint) natural yoghurt
grated rind of 1 orange
225 g (8 oz) apples
a little sugar or honey
6 teaspoons gelatine
6 tablespoons water
3 egg whites
175 g (6 oz) blackberries
250 ml ($\frac{1}{2}$ pint) double cream

Mix together the yoghurt and orange rind. Simmer the peeled apples in very little water, put them through a sieve and sweeten very lightly. Mix with two-thirds of the yoghurt and with 4 teaspoons of gelatine dissolved in 4 tablespoons warm water until syrupy. Beat 2 egg whites stiffly and fold them into the apple mixture. Pour this into two 15-cm (6-in) cake tins and freeze. Repeat the process using the blackberries and remaining yoghurt, gelatine, water and egg white, and freeze in one 15-cm (6-in) cake tin. When the 'cakes' are solid, turn out and sandwich together with whipped cream to make a tiered ice-cake, using a little cream to decorate the top. Serve at once.

Eggs

Well-fed, happy free-range chickens produce marvellous eggs with firm whites and rich yellow yolks, totally different from the battery variety. Eggs make delicious and quick meals, and with chickens and vegetables in the garden, self-sufficiency is almost in sight. Everyone knows about boiled, poached, fried and scrambled eggs, but omelettes and soufflés are easy and nourishing too. Curried hard-boiled eggs are excellent, particularly if vegetables are included in the sauce, and so are stuffed eggs and pickled eggs for snacks. A good supply of eggs means real egg custards, economical savoury flans, inexpensive lemon curd, delicious sauces for vegetables, and home-baked cakes and biscuits.

Leftover yolks or whites need never be wasted. An extra egg yolk enriches pastry, scones and batters, cream sauces and soups, or may be added to scrambled eggs, custards or flans. A number of yolks may be poached hard in a bowl standing in simmering water, then sieved and used as a garnish for soups, salads and rice dishes. Spare egg whites may obviously be made into meringues, but extra ones may be whisked into a soufflé, or into a just-setting jelly, or made into a meringue-topping for milk puddings or for sweet flans. Egg whites may be used in place of whole eggs when coating food with egg and crumbs for frying, and whisked egg whites may also be used for extending whipped cream, or for lightening a mixture of fruit purée and cream. Both yolks and whites may be frozen for future use.

Storing Eggs

There is often a time when hens are laying heavily and it is an advantage to be able to preserve a supply for lean months. For general storage, a refrigerator is not necessary, but eggs should be kept with the narrower end pointed down, in a cool place away from strong-smelling foods such as fish or onions which can flavour the eggs. Traditionally, eggs were preserved for longer periods in a waterglass solution, but today's freezer provides more convenient storage.

Waterglass Method

Make up waterglass according to instructions on the tin and put into a large stone jar or a bucket. Add a few fresh eggs at a time when available, and store in a place where the container need not be moved. Eggs which have thin, rough or cracked shells should not be put in the waterglass, which will keep them for up to fifteen months, although there is little point in storing for such a long period.

Freezing Method

Eggs cannot be frozen in their shells, but they can be frozen as whole eggs, or as yolks and whites separately. Hard-boiled eggs cannot be frozen as they become leathery and unpalatable. Use fresh, top quality eggs, and pack them in small or large freezer containers according to how you will use them. Individual eggs can be frozen in ice-cube trays or plastic egg trays, but it is more useful to freeze four or six eggs together for a recipe.

To freeze *whole eggs*, mix them lightly with a fork without introducing too much air, and add $\frac{1}{4}$ teaspoon salt or $\frac{1}{2}$ teaspoon sugar for 4 eggs. Label carefully with quantity, and whether salt or sugar has been added. *Whites* need no pre-freezing treatment. *Yolks* should be mixed lightly with a fork, adding $\frac{1}{2}$ teaspoon salt or $\frac{1}{2}$ teaspoon sugar to 6 yolks. Be sure to make a note of whether salt or sugar was added. To use frozen eggs, thaw them in the unopened container in a refrigerator and use as fresh eggs. If they have been packed in larger quantities, they may be measured out with a spoon: $2\frac{1}{2}$ tablespoons frozen whole egg = 1 egg; $1\frac{1}{2}$ tablespoons frozen egg

white = 1 egg white; 1 tablespoon frozen egg yolk = 1 yolk.
Eggs will store in the freezer for 8 months.

Pickled Eggs

12 eggs
1 litre (2 pints) white vinegar
25 g (1 oz) pickling spice

Hard-boil the eggs, remove the shells and put the eggs into a wide-mouthed jar. Boil the vinegar and spice together for 10 minutes, strain and pour over the eggs while still hot, covering them by at least 1 cm ($\frac{1}{2}$ in) vinegar. The jar should be covered with an acid-resistant lid. These may be used after 14 days, but will keep for up to 6 months. They are excellent served with salad.

BREAD

Small flour-grinding mills for use in the kitchen are rather expensive and will take a long time to repay themselves. Small quantities of grain may be ground in an electric coffee mill or blender, but only a few ounces should be ground at a time to avoid damaging the blades or over-taxing the motor. If you want to buy flour for breadmaking, white strong plain flour is now available in most shops (ordinary household flour is not suitable for breadmaking). If you prefer brown bread, buy 100% stoneground wholemeal flour which contains the whole of the cleaned wheat-grain with nothing added or taken away. Other flours may be labelled 80% or 90% which means that they contain proportionately less of the whole grain. For a soft tender loaf, a mixture of wholemeal and white flours produces a better texture than the rather solid loaf which results from using only wholemeal flour.

The other important bread ingredient is yeast, which may be fresh or dried. Fresh yeast looks like putty and is easy to cream and use—it is worth buying a quantity if it is available as it can be frozen for future use. Dried yeast is convenient, although some people find it gives a rather 'beery' flavour to their bread. It will keep up to 6 months in a tightly-lidded tin, but its efficiency diminishes rapidly in storage if there is much air space in the container, and it is really better to buy 25-g (1-oz) packets which can be used quickly. If using a recipe which specifies fresh yeast, the quantity of dried yeast will be exactly half the fresh yeast, and it must be mixed and allowed to froth strongly before it is added to the flour and other ingredients.

Salt is important for yeast baking, giving a good flavour and preventing the yeast fermenting too quickly, but too much will kill the yeast. Sugar acts as a food for yeast, but too much kills some of the yeast cells and causes the rather 'beery' flavour so often associated with home-made bread. Fat enriches dough, increases loaf volume, improves the softness and colour of the crumb and delays staling. The liquid in bread may be milk, water or a mixture, and generally slightly less than 250 ml ($\frac{1}{2}$ pint) liquid to 450 g (1 lb) strong flour is a useful guide, but flours vary in the amount of liquid they absorb. The liquid must be lukewarm to start the yeast working.

Wholemeal Farmhouse Bread

1·35 kg (3 lb) 100% stoneground wholemeal flour
20 g ($\frac{3}{4}$ oz) sea salt
25 g (1 oz) butter
25 g (1 oz) yeast
750 ml (1$\frac{1}{4}$ pints) lukewarm water

Grease 4 450-g (1-lb) loaf tins. Put the flour and salt into a mixing bowl and rub in the fat. Add the yeast to the water and mix until dissolved, then stir into the flour. Mix to a soft dough and knead on a lightly floured surface for 5 minutes. Cover with a tea towel and leave in a warm place for about 30 minutes until the dough has doubled in size. Turn on to a floured surface and knead the bread again. Divide into four portions and shape to fit the greased tins. Cover and leave in a warm place until the dough has risen 1 cm ($\frac{1}{2}$ in) above the rim of the tins. Bake at 230°C (450°F)/Gas 8 for 20 minutes. Reduce heat to 220°C (425°F)/Gas 7 for 15 minutes. Turn on to a wire rack and cool.

Flowerpot Bread

175 g (6 oz) strong white flour
225 g (8 oz) wholemeal flour
2 teaspoons salt
15 g ($\frac{1}{2}$ oz) lard
2 teaspoons sugar
15 g ($\frac{1}{2}$ oz) fresh yeast
250 ml ($\frac{1}{2}$ pint) water

What could be more appropriate for a gardener than bread baked in a flowerpot? Loaves were originally baked on the floor of ovens without containers, but clay pots give a subtle and delicious flavour to the bread. Use new flowerpots, grease them well and bake them empty for 15 minutes in a hot oven a couple of times before use. Store them in the larder for use again. The best pots to use have 12·5-cm (5-in) diameter tops.

Mix the flours and salt in a bowl and rub in the lard. Mix the sugar into the flour. Mix the yeast with lukewarm water and add to the flour all at once. Mix to a soft dough which leaves the bowl clean, adding a little more flour if necessary. Knead the dough on a lightly floured surface for 3 minutes until smooth. Divide the dough in half and shape into well-greased flowerpots. Put inside a large, lightly oiled polythene bag loosely tied at the top, and leave in a warm place for about 30 minutes until the dough is double in size. This will take 1–1½ hours at average room temperature. Remove the bag and bake the loaves standing upright at 230°C (450°F)/Gas 8 for 35 minutes. Turn out on a wire rack and cool. For a special finish, brush the tops with a little salted water and sprinkle with cracked wheat (available from health food shops) just before baking.

Brown Soda Bread

100 g (4 oz) strong plain flour
350 g (12 oz) wholemeal flour
1 teaspoon salt
1 teaspoon sugar
1 teaspoon bicarbonate of soda
2 teaspoons cream of tartar (only when fresh milk is used)
15 g (½ oz) butter
250 ml (½ pint) buttermilk or sour milk or fresh milk

Put the flours, salt, sugar, soda and cream of tartar, if used, into a mixing bowl. Rub in the butter and mix to a soft dough with the milk. Turn on to a floured board and knead lightly to form a smooth dough without cracks. Flatten into a circle about 17·5 cm (7 in) in diameter and put on a floured baking sheet. Brush with a little beaten egg or milk, or a mixture of both, and slash a cross on top with a sharp knife. Bake at 200°C (400°F)/Gas 6 for 40 minutes. Cool on a wire rack. This is a quick and easy bread if yeast is not available.

Index